WEIRD PLACES *IN* ATLANTIC CANADA

Humorous, Bizarre, Peculiar & Strange
Locations & Attractions across the Provinces

WEIRD PLACES IN ATLANTIC CANADA

Humorous, Bizarre, Peculiar & Strange Locations & Attractions across the Provinces

Andrew Fleming

BLUE
BIKE
BOOKS

The Publisher: Blue Bike Books
Website: www.bluebikebooks.com

Library and Archives Canada Cataloguing in Publication

Fleming, Andrew, 1972
   Weird places in Atlantic Canada : humorous, bizarre, peculiar & strange locations & attractions across the provinces / Andrew Fleming.

Includes bibliographical references.
ISBN 978-1-897278-59-8

   1. Atlantic Provinces—Miscellanea. 2. Atlantic provinces—Description and travel—Miscellanea. I. Title.

FC2005.F59 2009   971.5   C2009-900195-0

Project Director: Nicholle Carrière
Project Editor: Jordan Allan
Cover Image: "Bay of Fundy at Low Tide," Daryl Benson
Illustrations: Peter Tyler, Roger Garcia, Patrick Hénaff, Pat Bidwell and
   Graham Johnson

We acknowledge the support of the Alberta Foundation for the Arts for our publishing program.

We acknowledge the financial support of the Government of Canada through the Book Publishing Industry Development Program (BPIDP) for our publishing activities.

 Canadian Heritage   Patrimoine canadien

PC: 1

CONTENTS

DEDICATION

For Carmen Alatorre

INTRODUCTION

When the going gets weird, the weird turn pro.

–Hunter S. Thompson

"Weird" is one of those words with some wiggle room. Just as the word "funny" can mean either "funny ha ha" or "funny peculiar," "weird" can be a good thing or a bad thing depending on the context and your personal outlook. Which is just as well when you're writing a book entitled *Weird Places in Atlantic Canada*—it leaves plenty of room for interpretation. One person's weird is another person's wonderful.

According to the *Canadian Oxford Dictionary*, the word "weird" means "strange, unusual, out of the ordinary, and bizarre." However, the story of how this definition came to be commonly accepted is a bit, well, *weird* in its own right, seeing as the word once had a different meaning entirely.

"Wyrd" was originally a concept in Old English and Norse culture—similar to fate or karma—that was associated with The Fates, the three sibling goddesses who controlled human destiny. Common to various European mythologies, the three sisters were known as the Moirae to the Greeks, the Norn to the Germans and the Parcae to the Romans. Wyrd, in a nutshell, refers to how the past affects the future and the future affects the present, and hints at how all things are weirdly connected somehow.

However, the term itself only really entered the lingua franca and took on a weird life of its own after William Shakespeare penned the prophetic Weird Sisters into his play *Macbeth*. The three sisters not only gave accurate (albeit highly cryptic) predictions of the future, but they were usually portrayed as odd or just plain creepy-looking, which is how the word came to have the meaning it does today. According to the play, the three soothsaying sisters even sported beards, which you have to admit is pretty weird even in the days well before electrolysis.

While there is an example of old-school weirdness in this book about how, in 1868, a guy named Stephen Saxby was able to predict a deadly storm —now called "the Saxby Gale"—a full year in advance, most of the other examples in this book are considered to be on the strange side for a wide variety of reasons. Weirdness, like beauty, is in the eye of the beholder, but hopefully most readers will agree that a place whose tourist attractions include such things as flaming ghost ships, giant lake monsters, sub-zero surfing, a headless nun and annual giant pumpkin boat races are more than just passing strange.

Atlantic Canada is an odd place. It is a place where rivers run upstream and cars roll uphill. It is a place where two of the three biggest cities have nearly identical names. It is where dried seaweed is considered a delicacy, where parties usually take place in the kitchen and where nobody is in the least bit offended that the locally filmed hit television series *Trailer Park Boys* passes itself off as a documentary.

A bit beaten up by centuries of economic collapses, tragedies at sea, political boondoggles, sectarian violence and mining disasters, this weather-beaten part of Canada is its oldest and, arguably, its most interesting region.

Mystifying Mysteries of Atlantic Canada

Eastern Canada is a place of magic and wonder, and it is full of mysteries that science may never understand. However, it also has its fair share of idiots who make things up just to draw attention to themselves. Some of the region's more intriguing mysteries include evidence that suggests other explorers from Europe—and possibly even Asia— may have landed in Canada centuries before anyone else. Some believe the area has even been visited by visitors from outerspace and Jesus Christ himself.

SENT TO AN EARLY GRAVE
L'ANSE AMOUR, LABRADOR

The oldest-known grave in all of North America can be found on the Strait of Belle Isle coast in southern Labrador. Many moons ago, around 7500 years worth, a culture known as the Maritime Archaic people elaborately buried a 12-year-old boy in a broad pit in the sand.

The boy's body was wrapped in a shroud of bark and placed face down, with his head pointing to the west and a slab of rock placed across his back. A cache of knives, spear points and a walrus tusk were placed near his head, and close to one of his hands a whistle made from the hollow bone of a bird was uncovered. Huge bonfires were lit on either side of the grave.

Nobody knows if the boy was somebody particularly important or if the elaborate burial—unlike any other known gravesite of this primitive society—held some other special significance. Some anthropologists have suggested that the ceremonial burial could have been motivated by superstition, perhaps on account of strange environmental conditions that threatened the group's survival, such as a lack of winter ice that would've made seal hunting impossible. The ritual burial may have even been some sort of sacrificial offering, a plea to the spirit world for divine intervention. Or maybe there are thousands of similar burial sites throughout Labrador, and this happens to be the only one discovered so far—in that case, only time will tell.

TOUCH OF THE IRISH
GREAT NORTHERN PENINSULA, NEWFOUNDLAND

In ancient times, hundreds of years before the dawn of history,
Lived a strange race of people: the Druids.
No one knows who they were or what they were doing
But their legacy remains, hewn into the living rock.

–Spinal Tap, "Stonehenge"

We tend to look down on the people who lived several centuries ago, what with their marriages to their cousins, crummy mud hovels and poor standards of personal hygiene. But we have to give credit where it's due: they left behind some weird artifacts that have left the brightest of modern minds scratching their noggins in confusion.

Take, for example, Newfoundland's so-called "Ogham Stone." Located near the tip of the Great Northern Peninsula, this car-sized boulder is inexplicably covered with rune-like markings resembling Ogham, the secret script used by the ancient Druids. The etchings themselves are covered in a particularly slow-growing strain of lichen that botanically guarantees them to be at least several hundred years old.

Some believe the Ogham Stone is proof that early seafaring Irish monks possibly led by the legendary Saint Brendan the Navigator (484–577) established a colony in the late fifth century, nearly a millennia before Columbus sailed the ocean blue in 1492 and "discovered" North America.

Further evidence to support this theory is based on the fact that a line drawn on a globe between the 51st and 52nd degrees of north latitude would pass directly through the Newfoundland site as well as other Druidic hotspots such as Stonehenge, Avebury and Ireland's Dingle Peninsula—the point from which Brendan initially set off in his tiny leather boat on a mission to spread the word of God to the western world.

Nobody knows the actual fate of Saint Brendan but they didn't call him "the Navigator" for nothing, and if there was anybody who could've made it all the way to the shores of Atlantic Canada way back then, it was him. In 1976, author Tim Severin and companions proved that such a traverse was possible by building an exact replica of the wood-and-leather *curragh* used by Brendan and successfully sailing from

Ireland to Newfoundland without the assistance of nautical maps or modern technology.

Or maybe the mysterious stone, located just 20 kilometres south of L'Anse aux Meadows, is some sort of practical joke left behind by the Vikings. While popular myth unfairly paints them as bloodthirsty raiders fond of raping and pillaging, the Vikings were highly accomplished explorers in their own right—the Norse visited the northeast coast of North America several centuries before the likes of John Cabot or Samuel de Champlain.

DID YOU KNOW?

According to *The Saga of Eric the Red*, Leif "the Lucky" Eriksson first set foot in Newfoundland about 1000 AD,

four centuries after the supposed landing of Saint Brendan.
Eriksson is thought to have landed here after being blown
off course while trying to return home to Norway from
Greenland. He named the newfound land Vinland for its
abundance of wild grapes. Others soon followed and established a settlement near L'Anse aux Meadows, which was
discovered in 1961 when Norwegian archeologists Helge
and Anne Stine—after interviewing local fishermen and
being told of unusual mounds in the area—tracked the site
down. L'Anse aux Meadows is now a UNESCO World
Heritage site.

THE PEOPLE UNDER THE STAIRS
MOCKBEGGAR, NEWFOUNDLAND

If you ever saw the classic '80s horror film *Poltergeist*, you
would know it's never a good idea to build a house on top
of ancient burial grounds. And though no Mockbeggar
children were sucked into television sets or attacked by
angry elm trees, there is still a strange local tale surrounding
a cemetery that was discovered underneath local houses.

The story goes that toward the end of the 19th century
a heavy storm knocked down several houses in this small
community on Bonavista Bay.

When workers began digging through the wreckage, they
unearthed a series of coffins made of a type of wood not
found anywhere in Newfoundland. The coffins were held
together with wooden pegs rather than nails, which suggested that they dated back to the 1700s at the earliest.

Things got even weirder when the workers cracked the
coffins open. The bodies inside were extremely well pre-
served—likely the result of being buried in compact mud
rather than soil—and the dead men, women and children

were wearing drab grey clothing similar to what the Puritans wore. However, since there is no record of Puritans ever landing on the Rock, some speculated that the bodies must be the remains of French fishermen who had been visiting the Bonavista Bay area for centuries. The problem with this theory is that the French reportedly never brought their families with them on the dangerous fishing trips, or for that matter ever established any kind of permanent settlements.

The mystery of the mud cemetery has never been solved. Local legend has it that, on stormy nights similar to the one that brought the coffins back to the surface in the first place, you can hear the sound of someone singing in a foreign language coming from the site.

THE LEGLESS WONDER
DIGBY NECK, NOVA SCOTIA

It's only a flesh wound!

–The Black Knight, *Monty Python and the Holy Grail*

A narrow strip of land on the eastern shore of the Bay of Fundy is the site of one of Canada's strangest and most enduring mysteries.

One summer day in 1863, residents of Digby Neck noticed a large ship mysteriously tacking back and forth out at sea. At the time, nobody thought too much about it, but the mystery deepened the following day when a local fisherman in nearby Sandy Cove spotted what he thought was a large otter laying on the beach—only it wasn't an otter. Instead, he came across a nearly dead young man with no legs.

Not only was the stranger conspicuously lacking his lower appendages, but his legs had only recently been amputated—and by a skilled hand at that. Whoever had done the deed had then taken care to thoroughly bandage the man's stumps and had left him on the beach with some bread and a bottle of water.

When the man regained consciousness, the townspeople were obviously quite curious as to who he was and how he had got there. They never did find out. Instead, the man never said a word; he was either deaf or mute, or deaf *and* mute or was simply pretending for reasons of his own. The man was estimated to be around 19 years old, had soft hands—suggesting a life of leisure—and was dressed in expensive clothes with their tags removed. He was also well-nourished and, apart from the whole no-legs-and-no-communication-skills thing, was in otherwise excellent physical condition.

The townspeople had little choice but to take the helpless man under their care, naming him Jerome after a guttural noise he had once made when they asked him his name.

Local speculation was that Jerome had attempted to lead a mutiny and, instead of being keel-hauled or forced to walk the plank, double amputation had been his punishment. Others thought that he must have been the heir to some sort of glorious fortune and had been crippled and cast away in order to make room for someone else to claim it. One time, two women from the United States apparently visited Jerome and met with him privately, but they left abruptly without explaining to anyone else why they'd come.

Jerome spent the rest of his life boarding with local families in the area, sitting by fires when it was cold and hanging out with the cows in the barn, or watching the kids play when it was warm.

Whoever he was, he took his secret to his grave with him, buried under a modest tombstone in the Meteghan cemetery that simply states: Jerome, 1912.

UFOS, EH!

SHAG HARBOUR, NOVA SCOTIA

*The only thing that can unite mankind
is a threat from outer space.*

–Ronald Reagan

An otherwise unremarkable Nova Scotia fishing village in Shelburne County, Shag Harbour is famous for being the site of the world's only government-acknowledged Unidentified Flying Object crash.

"The Incident," as it is referred to in this neck of the woods, refers to the unexplained occurrence of October 4, 1967, in which several witnesses—including three RCMP officers and an Air Canada pilot—reported seeing strange blinking lights hovering in the sky before a large object appeared to plunge into the ocean, accompanied by a bright flash and a loud explosion. The ship splash-landed only a kilometer from shore and horrified witnesses watched as the shape floated for several minutes before finally sinking.

Convinced a plane had just crashed, local residents jumped into their fishing boats to look for survivors. Instead, what they found was weird fluorescent-yellow foam floating on the surface that smelled like sulfur and evaporated when they tried to collect it. Even weirder, neither the Rescue Coordination Centre in Halifax nor the nearby NORAD radar facility had any knowledge of a missing or crashed aircraft.

Before long, the navy, air force, Coast Guard and RCMP were all on the scene, and they searched for several days before also coming up empty-handed. Today, the mystery of the UFO endures and has earned Shag Harbour the reputation for being Canada's version of Roswell.

Shag Harbour is also somewhat famous for its unintentionally funny name. The town takes its name from an old French word for the cormorant—a type of diving bird—but "shag" means something else entirely in most English-speaking countries outside of North America, which is how the Austin Powers film title *The Spy Who Shagged Me* managed to sneak past the censors.

Of course, alien abductions are notorious for including anal probes, so maybe some inexperienced little green men were out looking for a close encounter with some Shag Harbour bluenosers before their ship accidentally crashed.

DID YOU  KNOW?

While it is the most famous, the Shag Harbour incident is far from the only reported sighting of a UFO in Atlantic Canada. As recently as Boxing Day of 2008, a PEI couple out for a stroll with their video camera shot footage of a mysterious object trailing a huge plume of smoke as it slowly plummeted into the Northumberland Strait. Neither Environment Canada nor the Transportation Safety Board of Canada can say what it was exactly that Tony and Marie Quigley captured on their camera, and once again there is no record of any listed aircraft going missing. You can draw your own conclusions by watching the strange recording at www.ufocasebook.com/123107.html.

MIRACLE ON HIGHWAY 105
BRAS D'OR, NOVA SCOTIA

Give us this day our daily bread.

–Matthew 6: 9–13

It is said that the Lord works in mysterious ways, which is probably as good an explanation as any as to why He might choose to make an appearance at a Tim Horton's drive-thru in Cape Breton. It certainly would have been just as mysterious, not to mention funnier, if He'd chosen the A&K Lick-A-Chick restaurant a few doors down instead.

In any case, back in 1998 a devout doughnut enthusiast spotted what she felt certain was the face of Jesus H. Christ Himself on the exterior brick wall of a Tim Horton's and, before you could say "Praise the Lord and pass the apple fritters," the fast-food franchise outlet on the outskirts of Sydney found itself flooded by flocks of the faithful (not to mention the merely curious) looking for a side of double take with their double-doubles.

But Jesus, being such a busy guy, didn't stick around the Timmy Ho's for long. The image disappeared just as suddenly as it appeared, though a skeptic might suggest the installation of new outdoor lights may have played a part in the Lord's vanishing act. Or maybe His schedule simply had Him slated to appear on a potato chip next, or a grilled cheese sandwich, or perhaps the side of a cow somewhere.

MADE UP CHINA
CAPE DAUPHIN, NOVA SCOTIA

There is a mountain in eastern Cape Breton that some people believe contains the remains of an ancient Chinese civilization. Not many of those people are archeologists, mind you, but it is still a heck of an interesting theory.

In 2002, architect Paul Chiasson was hiking through the woods on remote Cape Dauphin when he came across the remains of an ancient-looking road. Fairly wide and from all appearances bordered at one time by expertly cut stone walls, the thoroughfare had obviously been a major undertaking. Chiasson followed the road to its terminus and came upon what appeared to be platform foundations, suggesting the remains of an ancient settlement.

After spending most of the next two years in libraries researching the history of European exploration in North America, Chiasson came to the conclusion that the settlement couldn't possibly have been made by the Portuguese, the French, the English, the Norse, the Scots or any of the other usual suspects.

In his book *The Island of Seven Cities: Where the Chinese Settled When They Discovered America*, Chiasson presents the radical theory that Cape Breton is the legendary "Island of Seven Cities" mentioned in the writings of early European explorers and that 600 years or so ago Chinese settlers established a bustling city on this remote mountaintop. After all, if you were to dig a tunnel straight down from China and through the earth, you'd end up in North America, so anything could be possible.

His most compelling argument is the supposed Chinese stamp left on local Mi'kmaq culture. Not only are they the only North American native tribe to develop a written language of their own, but many of the characters they employ bare a striking resemblance to Chinese calligraphy. Mi'kmaq clothing, technical can-do and mythology also show many seemingly "made in China" similarities.

Chiasson's book caused a fair bit of hubbub when it came out in 2006 and attracted the attention of David Christianson, the curator of archeology at the Nova Scotia Museum. He and four other archeologists headed to the site and, after examining the "ancient ruins," came to a drastically different conclusion: there had never been any human settlement in the area, Chinese or otherwise. The so-called "foundations" of the city were simply flat rocks that can be

found elsewhere in the Cape Breton Highlands, and the reason that the construction of the mysterious road appeared to be so technically advanced is because it was worked on as recently as 1989 by a construction crew using bulldozers to build a firebreak on the mountain.

Haunted Places in Atlantic Canada

It is a damned ghost that we have seen...

–William Shakespeare, *Hamlet*

They're heeeeeeeere!

–Carrol Anne Freeling, *Poltergeist*

As one of the oldest inhabited places in North America, Atlantic Canada is also one of the continent's most haunted. There are said to be more ghosts here than you can shake a stick at (not that shaking sticks at ghosts is recommended) and trying to list them all would require several books. In fact, more diligent authors than I have compiled such books, and I'm thoroughly indebted to them for their expertise.

I once hiked out to a place called Partridge Island, which is connected to the city of Saint John by an old stone break-water. The island, now abandoned, was where thousands of Irish refugees trying to escape the Potato Famine found themselves quarantined after arriving in Canada, having been deemed "too sick" to be allowed entry. After submitting to a brutal kerosene shower, the sickly refugees were forced to wait and see if they would get better. Most didn't and hundreds of people died on the island over the years and were buried in unmarked graves.

While exploring the island, I remember peeking through the window of one of the empty buildings and being spooked by the sight of two spectral figures staring back at me. After picking myself back up off the ground and waiting for my breathing to return to normal, I plucked up the courage to take a second look, fully expecting the ghosts to have vanished into thin air.

As it turned out, what I had mistook for ghosts were actually just black-and-white cardboard cutouts of two people dressed in historical clothing that were probably left behind from some misguided attempt to turn the island into a park or tourist attraction.

But while I've never seen a ghost while in Atlantic Canada, I certainly wouldn't rule out the possibility—especially when visiting some of the following places.

HEADLESS TALE
ST. JOHN'S, NEWFOUNDLAND

The first reported ghost story in North America was of a headless man walking the streets of Newfoundland's capital city, a report made nearly a century before Washington Irving created his classic Headless Horseman in the short story "The Legend of Sleepy Hollow."

Back in 1745, a fellow named Samuel Pettyham was returning to his home on Queen's Road in a carriage when the horse suddenly stopped and refused to go any farther. Impatient, Pettyham got out and decided to walk the rest of the way. It was dark and when he spotted what appeared to be a man carrying a lantern, he hurried over to meet him. When the stranger stepped into the moonlight, however, Pettyham was confronted by a tall man with no head. Escaping to a nearby boarding house, Pettyham vowed to never spend another night in his home again.

The headless wanderer is thought to be the spirit of a murdered sea captain who used to live at the same address as Pettyham. The story goes that he was involved with a beautiful local woman who, while the captain was away at sea, would spend her time in the arms of another man. One fateful night, said other man ambushed his rival as he was returning home, jumping from the shadows and chopping off the captain's head with a sword.

They say the killer was never brought to justice and now the headless captain's ghost, having been spotted countless more times over the centuries, is unable to rest. Maybe he can't find the right kind of pillow?

THE LAST DUEL
St. John's, Newfoundland

They say that the loser of one of the last duels ever fought in Canada still haunts St. John's today and that his ghost restlessly roams the city looking for a rematch.

Once upon a time, Ensign John Philpot and Captain Mark Rudkin were both vying for the affections of a comely young lass named Colleen, the daughter of a prominent St. John's citizen. On March 30, 1826, the situation came to a head during a game of cards when Philpot accused his rival of cheating and threw water in his face.

The two agreed to draw pistols at dawn, as you did in those days, meeting at the foot of Robinson's Hill. When the signal came to start the duel Rudkin, an expert marksman, fired into the air in the hopes of settling things peacefully while Philpot's shot grazed the collar of Rudkin's coat. It was *on*. They reloaded and this time Rudkin, not one to miss, shot to kill.

Despite his initial intentional misfire, Rudkin found himself charged with murder in the first degree. After a swift trial, the jury returned with a guilty verdict, but the Chief Justice refused to accept it and sent them back to deliberate further. Twenty minutes later, the jury returned with a not guilty verdict and that was the end of it.

Rumour has it that Ensign Philpot still haunts the foggy streets of Newfoundland's capital. In the years since, numerous people have reported seeing a man waving a pistol at the foot of the hill where Philpot met his end.

HAUNTED SEAS

SHIP OF GHOULS

BAIE-DES-CHALEURS, NEW BRUNSWICK

Tales of the phantom ship, from truck to keel in flames;
She sails the wide Northumberland Strait,
No one knows her name.
Tales of the phantom ship, it's a ship of fire they cry;
Hard against the wind she sails,
No one can say why.

–Lennie Gallant, "Tales Of The Phantom Ship"

For several centuries now, witnesses have reported seeing a three-masted, flaming ship sailing in the waters of Northumberland Strait, particularly in and around the Baie-des-Chaleurs. The spooky sight has been spotted from every village on both sides of the strait, and several stories have been concocted to explain the phenomenon. The most credible one involves two brothers, Gaspar and Miguel Corte-Real, Portuguese explorers who visited the area in the 1500s while searching for the elusive Northwest Passage to Asia.

Gaspar was the first of the two to voyage to the New World, where he traded cheap booze and knick-knacks to the Mi'kmaq in exchange for their valuable furs. One dark day, he invited a group of around 60 native men aboard his ship for a feast featuring all the whisky they could drink. When the men woke the next morning, they found themselves not only badly hung over but also chained below deck and bound for Portugal, where they were eventually sold into slavery.

Gaspar unwisely decided to try his luck with this trick again a few years later and he returned a second time, only this time the

Mi'kmaq weren't as naïve. When he arrived back at the Baie-des-Chaleurs, they boarded Gaspar's ship under a moonless sky and captured the traitor following a bloody battle with his crew.

Mi'kmaq legend has it that justice was served to Gaspar Corte-Real by tying him to a heavy rock at low tide, which afforded him a drawn-out death by drowning when the tide came back in.

A few years later, Miguel Corte-Real is said to have come looking for his missing brother. Recognizing his ship still at anchor, Miguel and his men boarded the vessel to investigate. They too were attacked by Mi'kmaq warriors who, after another bloody battle, succeeded in setting the ship on fire, killing all hands on board.

Some say the two Portuguese brothers have been haunting the local seas ever since; others say the so-called "fire ship" is instead simply an optical illusion caused by gaseous vapours from undersea coal beds breaking through the surface of the ocean. If you spend enough time hanging out on the beaches of the Northumberland Straight, maybe you can decide for yourself.

THAR SHE BLOWS UP!
MAHONE BAY, NOVA SCOTIA

Smoke on the water, a fire in the sky

–Deep Purple, "Smoke On The Water"

The Northumberland Strait isn't the only body of water said to have a flaming ship sailing its seas. People have reported seeing yet another fiery phantom ship in the waters of Mahone Bay ever since a schooner named *The Young Teazer* went down in flames two centuries ago.

The doomed ship was under the command of Lieutenant Frederick Johnston, an American privateer who unwisely

brought the War of 1812 to the waters of Nova Scotia. Johnston had already been captured by the British once before and was only released after solemnly swearing to never bear arms against the Crown again. He must've had his fingers crossed when he made that promise because, after he was escorted back to Maine, he promptly hit the high seas again in *The Young Teazer* and commandeered five more British vessels.

This development did not go over too well with the Brits, who responded by sending several Royal Navy ships in pursuit of Johnston and eventually cornered *The Young Teazer* in St. Margarets Bay.

Well aware that he would be executed if recaptured, Johnston decided to fall on his proverbial sword. Or, more accurately, he set the *Teazer*'s ammunitions stores on fire and blew his entire ship and crew out of the water—all hands, save eight, were lost, including Johnston.

A year later, locals began to report sightings of a ship burning on the horizon. Whenever rescue boats were sent out to investigate, however, the burning ship would mysteriously vanish. Fishermen have also been surprised by a blazing ship that appears out of nowhere and nearly runs them down. Those who have seen the ship up close also claim to have seen panicked men screaming and running around on deck.

The flaming ship has become so engrained in the collective local imagination that the event is paid tribute to each summer as part of the Mahone Bay Classic Boat Festival. The Royal Navy's pursuit is re-enacted by having two ships simulate a naval gun battle and, after they disappear from view, igniting a huge explosion that colours the horizon.

GENII AT THE BOTTOM
NEW RIVER BEACH, NEW BRUNSWICK

They say that the ghost of a drowned sailor walks along a stretch of sandy beach in southern New Brunswick on foggy nights. The speculation is that he could be one of the 11 men who died when their ship, the *Genii*, sank during the infamous Saxby Gale of 1869 (see Weird Weather).

The *Genii*, which was loaded with lumber and bound for Liverpool, was moored behind a breakwater when the tempest struck, but even the breakwater couldn't prevent the ship from taking on water and sinking to the bottom. Most of the drowned bodies were found right away, but one took several days longer to resurface, finally washing up on what is now New River Beach Provincial Park, several kilometres from the wreck of the *Genii*.

Along with the oft-spotted male ghost sadly strolling along the sand, a female ghost has also been reported, possibly the wife of one of the local sailors who is searching restlessly for her lost love. The house where the bodies of the dead sailors were laid out has also been the site of some supposedly paranormal occurrences, including strange sounds and disembodied footsteps.

HAUNTED WOODS

HOME OF THE WHOOPER
NORTHUMBERLAND COUNTY, NEW BRUNSWICK

Since that day, so goes the word,
Fearful sounds have long been heard,
Far round the scene where lies the woodsman's grave,
Whoops the stoutest hearts to thrill,
Yells that warmest blood to chill,
Sends terror to the bravest of the brave.

–Michael Whelan, "The Ballad of the Dungarvon Whooper"

New Brunswick is perhaps the only place in the world—certainly the only province in Canada—to have a train named after a ghost. Known as the Dungarvon Whooper, the train once traveled between Newcastle and Fredericton, making its way through forests said to be haunted by a ghost of the same name.

Local legend has it that in the late-19th century there was a young cook who worked at a logging camp near the Dungarvon River in the northeastern part of the province. He was said to have had a mighty set of lungs that he would use in the morning to awaken the loggers for their breakfasts and again at night to sing songs by the campfire.

The cook's brain, however, apparently wasn't nearly as well developed as his lungs were because, despite logging camps' deserved reputation for attracting rough-and-tumble types, he apparently was always seen sporting a prominent money belt around his waist, one that had a considerably larger bulge than you might expect from a lumber camp cook.

One day the cook went out hunting with one of the other men. When they were out of earshot, the logger supposedly murdered him and hid the money belt in the woods.

The killer then returned to camp, claiming that they'd been attacked by a bear and that he'd been knocked out while the cook had been dragged away. Alas, after he regained consciousness, the freshly fallen snow had kept him from following the bear's trail.

A search party was sent out, but the cook was never seen again. Nor, for that matter, was the logger who had been out with him, who disappeared while the rest of the camp was out searching.

The loggers were awoken later that night by someone (or something) screaming bloody murder. The ear-splitting howls lasted for hours and reoccurred the following night, causing the spooked lumberjacks to pack up and leave for good.

Ever since, people in the area have reported hearing unnatural screams and howls coming from the woods. The cries became so bad that eventually a priest from nearby Renous was brought in to perform an exorcism.

Some have suggested the screams could just be mountain lions, notwithstanding the fact that the animals are supposedly extinct in this part of the country, while others think they could be the cries of a territorial Sasquatch. Less creative types say the story was simply made up to discourage children from venturing too far into the forest.

Whatever the case, unnatural screaming (or "whooping") has been reported as recently as the mid-1980s, when a spooked Torontonian promptly abandoned the summer cottage he'd been building in the woods after hearing the eerie howls. True or false, it hardly seems like the sort of thing you'd report if you were trying to sell some real estate.

NUN LEFT BEHIND
FRENCH FORT COVE, NEW BRUNSWICK

You might think that being married to the Lord would put you straight onto the stairway to heaven upon death, but this hasn't turned out to be the case for Sister Marie Inconnus, a nun that has been haunting the Miramichi area for more than a century after losing her head over some buried treasure.

Sister Marie came to New Brunswick from France in the mid-18th century to help take care of displaced Acadians, eventually working at a refugee camp near French Fort Cove where she was put in charge of a rather large fund that was established to pay for the camp's needs.

Fearing an imminent attack by the British, Sister Marie and two other women, both of whom died of scurvy not long afterwards, decided to bury the funds along with family heirlooms in an undisclosed location until the danger passed.

Late one night while the nun was crossing the bridge over Crow Brook, someone who most likely wanted to know where her booty was stashed viciously attacked her. Nobody knows whether she gave up the location or not—the treasure has never been found—but what is certain is that the poor nun was badly beaten and then brutally decapitated. Soldiers discovered Sister Marie's body the next morning but not her head, which was possibly thrown into the brook. The crime was never solved.

Although her remains were returned to France for burial, Sister Marie's spirit is said to still remain in French Fort Cove. Many late night visitors to this wooded area have reported being approached by a headless woman wearing a nun's habit who pleads for help finding her head.

DID YOU KNOW?

The sightings have been so frequent over the years that nowadays there are even "Headless Nun" tours departing at dusk in the hope of bumping into her. If ghost hunting for a heartbroken, headless nun sounds like your idea of a good time, call 1-800-459-3131 to reserve a spot today!

IMMORTAL COMBAT
HEMLOCK RAVINE PARK, NOVA SCOTIA

The music rotunda, the only remaining structure of Prince's Lodge (the former estate of Edward the Duke of Kent), is still visible from Halifax's Bedford Highway. Back in July 1796, this rotunda was the site of a deadly duel, the outcome of which might still be undecided.

The Duke was hosting a large card party by the rotunda when an argument broke out between two of his officers—Colonel Ogilvie and Captain Howard—both of whom drew their swords and began fighting. Both men died from the battle, one on the spot and the other shortly afterwards from his wounds.

The Duke, thoroughly unimpressed by their behaviour, denied both men proper military funerals and instead had them buried in unmarked graves in the nearby woods.

Many years later, when a railway was being built through the Lodge's grounds, workers were surprised when they suddenly unearthed two adult male skeletons lying next to each other. Ever since, people claim to have seen two men locked in a swordfight on the same spot, which nonetheless is now a popular hiking destination.

HAUNTED HOUSE OF GOD
CHARLOTTETOWN, PRINCE EDWARD ISLAND

Early in the wee hours of October 7, 1859, several residents of the island's capital were woken from their slumber by intermittent ringing coming from the bell tower in St. James Church. By the time the bell had tolled for a fifth time, two men who lived next door had dragged themselves out of bed to investigate.

Local folklore has it that, as the men stood together in front of the church, the bell rang for a sixth time and the doors suddenly swung open to reveal three glowing women dressed all in white. The bell then rang once more and the doors slammed shut.

The men tried to go to the women, but the doors were now locked. Peering through the windows, they claim to have seen one of the women mounting the stairs to the belfry.

The church's minister eventually showed up to find out what in God's name was going on. He produced a key to the door and the men went in to investigate, but by then the church was empty. As the men climbed the stairs to the tower, the bell rang for the eighth and final time but, after arriving at the top, they found the tower empty and the bell rope tied in its usual place, though the bell itself was still vibrating.

The next day, it was discovered that a passenger steamer named *Fairie Queen* failed to arrive as scheduled from Nova Scotia. The ship had sunk that very night, killing all eight passengers— three women and five men. Many people believe that the Saint James Church's bell tolled eight times that night to foretell the death of each passenger.

HAUNTED RESTAURANTS

FISHERMEN'S FRIEND
THE FIVE FISHERMEN, NOVA SCOTIA

It would almost be more surprising if the Five Fishermen res-taurant *wasn't* haunted. Long before the stately three-storey building in downtown Halifax began its current incarnation as a high-end seafood joint, the site served as a funeral parlour and as a result was involved in two of the worst tragedies in Atlantic Canada's history—the 1912 sinking of the *Titanic* and the Halifax Explosion of 1917. Both events resulted in dozens of bodies of people who died violent and unexpected deaths being stacked like cordwood inside the overwhelmed mortuary's walls.

The Five Fishermen runs the gauntlet in terms of ghostly goings-on. According to the restaurant's website, "many of the staff…are so used to odd occurrences that they wouldn't even bat an eye when a glass flies off a shelf with no one near." There have been reports (mostly by staff working alone after hours, but also from the occasional spooked diner) of every-thing from glasses flying off shelves, disembodied voices, peo-ple being tapped on the shoulder in an empty room, floating blobs of ectoplasm and faucets and stoves turning themselves on and off at random.

The most consistent report is of an elderly, bearded man wearing old-fashioned clothing and strolling around the place.

DID YOU  KNOW?

The building at 1740 Argyle Street is famous for far more than phantoms and fine fish dishes. Opened in December 1816, it was inaugurated as the First National School, the earliest school in the country where children could receive an education for free. Several decades later it became the Victorian College of Art, the first school of fine arts in Canada, and was run by none other than Anna Leonowens, better known as the globetrotting governess from the book *Anna and the King of Siam* and later the Broadway musical and film *The King and I*. The school eventually relocated across town and was renamed the Nova Scotia School of Art and Design; it is considered to be one of the best art schools in the country.

CELLAR DWELLER

THE CELLAR BAR AND GRILL, NOVA SCOTIA

Fortunately, the Five Fishermen isn't the only place where you stand a chance of having a potentially paranormal dining experience in the Halifax area. If you're not in the mood for seafood, you can try your luck at the Cellar Bar and Grill at 1516 Bedford Highway instead. Back at the end of 19th century, the land on which the restaurant now stands was farmland belonging to a politician named James Butler. They say that a young woman was brutally murdered in his barn, and while suspicion at first fell on Butler, the killer was never brought to justice.

Some say the young woman's spirit now wanders the restaurant and staff over the years have reported such strangeness as severe temperature drops, the sound of footsteps when nobody is there, rearranged kitchen utensils, transplanted furniture, unplugged electronics acting up and (more suspiciously) employees being clocked-in when they're not scheduled to work.

Adding more grist for the ghostly rumour mill, a rotting body washed up on shore behind the building in the mid-1980s and was only discovered after the stench came wafting through the restaurant walls. Unlike the Five Fishermen, this is not the sort of thing the restaurant owners try to capitalize on.

INTRIGUE OF GENTLEMEN
THE HALIFAX CLUB, NOVA SCOTIA

In 1862, a bunch of well-to-do Haligonians built themselves an exclusive gentlemen's club on Hollis Street. Although the Halifax Club has always been strictly members-only, at least one permanent resident is said to remain there uninvited.

There are two theories regarding who might be haunting the Halifax Club, rearranging the place settings and appearing over the shoulders of patrons looking into mirrors. One version says that the ghost is an unnamed former member who died of a heart attack while in the arms of a prostitute. To save face, his buddies took the body and laid it across the club's front stairs to make it look instead as though he died on his way into the club. The other story claims that the ghost is a disgruntled former employee who stabbed himself in front of several club members and then, for good measure, jumped out a third-storey window to his death.

AFTERLIFE OF BRIAN
CHEZ BRIAN, NEWFOUNDLAND

The Five Fishermen isn't the only former funeral home to become a restaurant said to still be occupied by restless spirits. Chez Brian was once a bistro located on St. John's Duckworth Street that has since gone out of business—perhaps in part because of its reputation for being haunted.

A woman who used to live above the eatery reported waking up one night, unable to move, only to find a man floating above her. She claimed that as she lay there paralyzed, the man placed coins over her eyes and seemed to be preparing her body for burial. Kitchen workers at Chez Brian also reported numerous sightings of a naked woman strolling the corridors with a huge autopsy scar down her torso, just the sort of thing to put diners off their food.

STRANGE BREWERY
HALIFAX, NOVA SCOTIA

You might've seen one of those whimsical Alexander Keith's beer commercials in which a series of guys go to seek advice from a talking bust of the ale's namesake, who invariably suggests a glass of his finest India Pale Ale to be the solution to all their problems.

As it turns out, there could be a nugget of verisimilitude behind these ads given that the iconic brew master and former mayor of Halifax is said to still haunt his former waterfront brewhouse. They say that "those who like it like it a lot," which may explain why Alexander Keith himself has stuck around so long after downing his final pint. Or maybe there's simply no beer in heaven.

In any case, workers at the historic brewery and popular tourist attraction (again, those who like it like it a *lot*) at 1496 Lower Street have made several reports of his seeing his ghost throughout the building—possibly stopping by to make sure the beer's quality is still up to snuff—and of hearing footsteps in empty rooms and hallways.

While his ghost may still walk the halls of the brewery he founded in 1820—one of North America's oldest—Alexander Keith's body is buried at Camp Hill Cemetery across from the Halifax Public Gardens. Keith's birthday (October 5) is often marked by drunks who visit his grave and reverently place empty cans and bottles on it.

HAUNTED HOTELS

THE FAIRMONT ALGONQUIN HOTEL

ST. ANDREWS, NEW BRUNSWICK

One of the grandest hotels in all of Atlantic Canada, the Fairmont Algonquin Hotel is also said to be its most haunted.

The towering mock-Tudor hotel overlooking the picturesque seaside town of St. Andrews was built in 1889, making it the first summer resort in Canada. Back in those days, soaking up some sun and seawater was considered to be a cure-all for all kinds of ailments and one of the Algonquin Hotel's most famous attractions was its saltwater baths, where water from nearby Passamaquoddy Bay was pumped in and stored in tanks in the hotel's attic, from which baths could be drawn.

The luxury hotel has been a retreat for the rich and famous for well over a century now, attracting such notables as Prime Minister Sir John A. MacDonald, railway baron William Van Horne, U.S. President Teddy Roosevelt, Prince Charles and Princess Diana (back when they were still an item), Jell-O Pudding Pops enthusiast Bill Cosby and author Stephen King—who is said to have based the haunted Overlook Hotel in his famous novel *The Shining* on the Algonquin Hotel.

While the Algonquin isn't known to be haunted by spooky identical twin girls and doesn't have a homicidal caretaker or elevators brimming with blood, it *does* have more than its fair share of ghosts haunting its halls. The most frequent sighting is of a talkative, elderly bellman that helps guests to their rooms but disappears before he can be tipped. Confused guests often try to leave him some cash at the front counter, only to be told there is nobody fitting that description on staff.

Other former hotel workers who seem unable to leave their jobs behind include a ghostly night watchman who rattles his keys along banisters during his patrols and a female dining room server who likes to rearrange the table settings.

In Room 473, also known as "The Bride's Room," one can often hear the sound of a woman sobbing. A young newlywed reportedly died here in the early 1900s, either of a broken heart or suicide, after being abandoned by her new husband.

Other random occurrences include doorknobs that turn by themselves, sink taps that turn on and off in the Library Bistro, unexplained lights shining from a permanently closed tower and the sound of children's laughter when none are staying at the hotel.

STEM TA STERN BED AND BREAKFAST

BRIDGETOWN, NOVA SCOTIA

This B&B on Bridgetown's Granville Street is said to be haunted by a man who hung himself in one of its rooms.

According to legend, a past owner of the inn had only just bought the place when she was awakened one night by a strange noise. While investigating, she passed an empty room but heard a distinct tapping noise coming from behind the door.

As she peeked inside, she was confronted with the sight of a man hanging from a noose, who then disappeared after she understandably began screaming. Not exactly the sort of tale you would make up if you'd just opened up shop and were trying to convince people to come and stay at your inn.

Other guests over the years claim to have encountered a man with a severely twisted neck roaming the hallway, or have seen him standing at a window. These sightings are usually accompanied by a sudden drop in temperature.

THE LAMPLIGHT HOTEL
Truro, Nova Scotia

The Lamplight shut out the lights for good nearly a century ago because apparently it was bad for business to have a resident ghost who liked to beat up the guests.

The story goes that on September 23, 1919, a soldier who had recently returned from the war was staying at the hotel with his wife. While standing on the balcony of his room, he was surprised to spot a war buddy down below and invited him up for a chat. Later, as the soldier was returning from the hotel saloon, he found his supposed friend in bed with his wife. Furious, he pulled out a gun and shot them both dead, then jumped out the third-storey window to his own death.

Exactly one year later, someone on the street reported hearing the sound of gunfire before seeing a man leap from the same balcony. And then things started getting seriously weird around the hotel: guests reported dresser drawers flying open and their contents being shredded in mid-air; workers said their trolleys would suddenly take off at high speeds and crash into walls; and one person reported waking up in the infamous room in the middle of the night and finding himself sharing the bed with a strange man and woman. The door then flew open and another man shot his spectral companions before all three suddenly vanished.

The final straw was when a man broke several bones after claiming to have been squeezed by unseen forces. The hotel closed its doors for good just a few hours after this event and remains abandoned to this day.

SMELLS LIKE TEEN SPIRIT
AMHERST, NOVA SCOTIA

One of the all-time spookiest poltergeist stories took place in an otherwise unremarkable rural Nova Scotia town in Cumberland County.

The year was 1876 and 18-year-old Esther Cox, despite having lost both her parents as a child, was living a fairly normal life much like any other small-town girl, sharing a crowded house on Princess Street with her extended family.

One August night, as she and her sister Jennie were sleeping in bed, Esther suddenly screamed and told her sister that a mouse was under the covers. However, no mouse could be found and so the girls eventually went back to sleep.

The following night, the two awoke again after hearing rustling sounds from a box underneath the bed. They opened it up and were spooked further when they found it to be empty.

This is where things started to get extremely strange for poor Esther in a series of events that became known as "The Great Amherst Mystery."

The next time the whole family was suddenly awakened in the middle of the night, it was to the sight of Esther having a choking seizure, during which her hair stood completely on end, her skin turned bright red and her limbs swelled up like balloons. The family heard three loud, unexplainable bangs, and Esther's strange seizures suddenly ceased.

Four nights later the same thing happened, ending again with the mysterious banging sounds. A local doctor named Carritte was brought in to examine Esther and was at her bedside when her bedclothes were suddenly flung across the room by invisible hands and there was once again the sound of loud banging. Dr. Carritte then reported hearing a scratching noise above him, like metal scraping plaster, and he looked up the see the following message being etched on the wall over her head: "Esther Cox you are mine to kill."

And that was just the beginning. From then on, all manner of unexplained attacks and general *X-Files* weirdness followed the unfortunate Esther wherever she went. Along with the nightly limb-swelling and skin-reddening choking sessions, loud slapping noises were sometimes heard, followed by the blooming of red handprints on Esther's face. Unexplained fires started in the house, furniture slammed itself into walls, pins would fly from their cushions and stick into her face and, on one occasion, a small knife flew from a neighbouring kid's hand and stabbed her in the back.

It is entirely possible the boy simply threw the knife at her on purpose since, by this point, she was effectively the town pariah and was suspected of being possessed by the devil. It didn't help her cause when she once tried escaping her demons by hiding inside a local church, only to have the loud banging start up until she was forced to leave.

The final straw came after she moved out of the haunted house and took a job working at a farm outside of town. Unfortunately for her, one of the farm's barns promptly burned to the ground and Esther found herself charged with arson. She was sentenced to four months in jail, but only served a quarter of her sentence because there were so many witnesses to the unexplained phenomena and there was lingering sympathy for the girl.

After going to prison, however, the attacks ended as abruptly as they began and Esther Cox was able to live the rest of her life in peace, maybe not exactly happily ever after but at least no longer regularly molested by a poltergeist. She went on to marry twice and had two sons.

It eventually emerged that Esther had been attacked and nearly raped by a man she'd been dating, a local shoemaker named Bob McNeal, who fled town immediately after she escaped from him and before the strange events began.

Whether the occurrences were actually the work of some malevolent, supernatural being or were the subconscious telekinetic manifestations of a traumatized teen—not unlike a real-life version of Stephen King's famous character Carrie—remain part of the Great Amherst Mystery's enduring intrigue.

REACHING NIRVANA
ANTIGONISH, NOVA SCOTIA

As I was going up the stair
I saw a man who wasn't there
He wasn't there again today
Oh, how I wish he'd go away!

–Hughes Mearns, "Antigonish"

What is likely the world's most famous poem about a ghost (or, at the very least, about a ghost on a staircase) was written about a supposedly haunted spiral staircase in the former Mount St. Bernard College at Saint Francis Xavier University. A scowling man—said to be the spirit of a disgraced local priest who drove a nun to her gravity-assisted suicide—has often been reported glaring at people as they climb up and down the stairs.

American poet Hughes Mearns was a student at Harvard University when he included the lines in a play called "The Psyco-ed" in 1899 after hearing a second-hand account of the spooky stairs. The short poem was then published on its own in 1922 as "Antigonish" and later set to music as "The Little Man Who Wasn't There," which became a hit song for the Glenn Miller Orchestra in 1939.

The quatrain has since become a veritable part of the zeitgeist, popping up in such diverse places as the Stephen King novel *Dreamcatcher*, the films *Identity*, *Being Cyrus* and *Velvet Goldmine*, an episode of *Star Trek: The Next Generation* and the DC superhero comic *Doom Patrol*.

The lines were also parodied in *Mad* magazine ("There was a man upon the stair / When I looked back, he wasn't there / He wasn't there again today / I think he's from the CIA"), adapted by David Bowie for the song "The Man Who Sold The World," famously covered by Nirvana ("We passed upon the stair / We spoke of was and when / Although I wasn't there / He said I was his friend") and even by a British Prime Minister's own labour minister eager to see his boss leave office ("In Downing Street upon the stair / I met a man who wasn't Blair / He wasn't Blair again today / Oh how I wish he'd go away").

Interesting Islands of Atlantic Canada

Atlantic Canada is a land of islands. Two out of the four Atlantic provinces are separated from the mainland by the sea—and that's not even counting Cape Breton, which technically is about as much a part of Nova Scotia as Labrador is a part of Newfoundland. Nova Scotia itself is only attached to New Brunswick by a narrow strip of land that prevents it from being a full-fledged island rather than a peninsula and, let's be honest, PEI is really more of a big ol' sand dune that has managed to pass itself off a province, the "Birthplace of Confederation" aside.

Simon and Garfunkle once boasted of being both a rock and an island, but Newfoundland actually is. And if Québec ever decides to separate, the whole damn place will find itself cut adrift from the rest of the country.

But it is the lesser-known islands that are among the most interesting. There's one that is inhabited entirely by hundreds of wild horses, another that is elaborately booby-trapped and quite possibly contains a fortune in buried pirate treasure and yet another that was inexplicably zapped from outer space. An American president lost his legs on one and nobody is quite sure if another one belongs to Canada or the United States. Not only is there an archipelago in the Gulf of St. Lawrence that belongs to a province that isn't even a part of Atlantic Canada, there are two more islands in Atlantic Canada that are technically not even a part of North America.

THE CALL OF BOOTY
OAK ISLAND, NOVA SCOTIA

One of Canada's oldest mysteries continues to this day on an unassuming small island in Nova Scotia's Mahone Bay.

Oak Island is famous for its so-called "money pit," an excavation site rumoured to contain buried treasure that has had money thrown into it for centuries in fruitless attempts to locate *what*, if anything, lies at the bottom of it. Speculation regarding what the supposed buried treasure might be ranges from Captain Kidd's hidden booty of Peruvian gold, to the original manuscripts of William Shakespeare, to various treasures belonging to the Knights Templar or the Freemasons, maybe even the Holy Grail. For all anyone knows, it could hide a shortcut to China.

The mystery began in 1795 after Daniel McGinnis and two other local teens stumbled upon a depression in the ground. Like most young men, they were always on the lookout for booty and were no doubt familiar with a local legend that claimed pirates had stashed their treasure on islands in Atlantic Canada. With visions of gold doubloons dancing in their heads, they began to dig. A layer of flagstones gave way to two wood platforms, the deepest being nearly nine metres down, but nothing else was found beneath them. Bummed out, they abandoned their quest.

Nine years later, McGinnis returned with more serious help to try and discover the island's buried secret. After digging down close to 30 metres, the team finally discovered a stone slab carved with unfamiliar symbols and figured they were getting close to the treasure. But when they returned the next morning, the shaft was two-thirds full of water—the result of what looked to be a sophisticated booby trap involving additional adjoining tunnels.

According to the legend, a university professor then translated the symbols on the stone slab as reading, encouragingly, "forty feet below two million pounds lie buried," though it is difficult to imagine why the makers of insanely complicated booby traps would go out of their way to encourage the people who were digging for their treasure.

In the years since, numerous treasure hunters have sunk personal fortunes and dug other parallel tunnels hoping to solve this cavernous conundrum. Six lives have been lost in the digging and *still* nobody has any idea what is down there, as all attempts have been invariably flooded. Cement vaulting, gold chains, wooden chests and numerous scraps of paper have all been brought to the surface, and radiocarbon dating suggests that whoever left them there did so sometime in the 16th century.

Oak Island's current owners, Dan Blankenship and David Tobias, have worked on the island since the 1960s. As recently as December 2003, they announced some "exciting developments" would be forthcoming, but nothing ever happened. The dig site is currently for sale, and the Oak Island Tourism Society is hoping that the government will step up and dig deeper, financially speaking, to solve the mystery once and for all.

CANADIAN CASTAWAY
ÎLE DES DÉMONS, LABRADOR

Daniel Defoe wrote the novel *Robinson Crusoe* in 1719 after hearing about the rescue of a Scottish sailor named Alexander Selkirk, who had been marooned for four years on an island in the south Pacific. No doubt it was a terrible ordeal, but at least Selkirk—along with other notable castaways such as the Swiss Family Robinson, the mutineers of the *Bounty*, Green Arrow, Tom Hanks and his volleyball Wilson, and even Madonna— had the good fortune of being stranded on tropical islands, whereas poor young Marguerite de La Rocque found herself stuck on a cold, barren rock somewhere off the coast of Labrador for three long years.

After Jacques Cartier returned to France with tales of the unimaginable wealth to be found in what is now Atlantic Canada, Jean-François de La Rocque, the Sieur de Roberval, decided to set sail and see it for himself. He invited his 16-year-old niece Marguerite to join him, who jumped at the opportunity for reasons that had nothing to do with wanting to see the world. Young Marguerite was in love with a man named Pierre but her suitor had been deemed unsuitable by her father, and so she convinced her lover to stowaway on board so that they could be legally wed when they reached the New World—or maybe she just wanted some action during the long weeks at sea.

In any event, after setting sail in 1542, Marguerite and Pierre were caught together and her uncle, not exactly what you might call the "romantic type," ordered the two—along with Marguerite's complicit nurse—to be left ashore at the first sight of land, which happened to be the dreaded "Île des Démons," said to be inhabited by evil spirits who attacked anyone who tried to settle there.

For three summers and two unimaginably long winters, Marguerite managed to stay alive on the remote island. Her nurse was the first to die, followed by Marguerite's newborn child and eventually Pierre as well, before Marguerite was rescued by a passing fishing vessel—alerted by a last-ditch bonfire she lit with what was left of her wood supply—that took their chances in approaching the wild woman dressed in furs running up and down the supposedly haunted shore.

For those who believe in karma, you'll be happy to know that things didn't work out so well for her cruel uncle either. The unsuccessful voyage ruined the Sieur de Roberval and, after returning to France with his tail between his legs, he was eventually killed in a street fight. But not before his niece returned home again, which must have made for some excruciatingly awkward family dinners.

DID YOU KNOW?

Adding to the strange tale, nobody is entirely sure where the Île des Démons is actually located. Maps from the 1500s show it as two islands in the Gulf of Saint Lawrence, but the islands had mysteriously disappeared from maps drawn less than a century later. But judging from Marguerite's account of her time there, it is likely the legendary demons that attacked anyone who set foot on the island were probably just hungry mosquitoes.

THE STINK OF EXTINCTION
FUNK ISLAND, NEWFOUNDLAND

An isolated, uninhabited island approximately 60 kilometres off the northeast coast of Newfoundland, Funk Island got its name for the literal definition of funk—meaning a nasty, intolerable smell—rather than for being a cool, funky destination, such as Funkytown.

The source of the stink that gave the island its name was left by its former fowl occupants, the great auks (*Pinguinis impennis*)—a species of bird resembling a penguin that has since gone the way of the dodo—who left behind an enduring legacy of poop particularly rich in strong-smelling nitrates and phosphates.

The great auks had the great misfortune of not only having attributes useful to humans, but also—because of their inability to fly and their clumsiness on land—being extremely easy to kill. Early sailors and settlers made frequent forays to Funk Island to round up the hapless birds, simply herding them up their ships' gangplanks to make them into down-lined pillows and mattresses, lamp oil and meals that tasted like chicken.

The island was once home to tens of thousands of great auks; today there are exactly zero. The last sighting of this species came from off the coast of Iceland on June 3, 1844, by naturalists who stumbled across a nesting pair and, naturally, killed them and took their eggs.

Although the Funk's auks are now deader than disco, the island continues to live up to its funky name thanks to brand-new layers of bird guano deposited by its new tenants, the thin-billed murres (*Uria aalge*), which have a population estimated at 400,000 pairs on Funk Island.

FIVE FOR FIGHTING
GRAND MANAN ISLAND, NEW BRUNSWICK

The largest island in the Bay of Fundy, this sleepy fishing community with a population of around 2500 takes its name from mixing the French word *grand*, meaning "big," with the Maliseet word *munanook*, meaning "island." Fittingly, the island is reasonably big. Samuel de Champlain first recorded the island's name as Menane and the prefix Grand was added later to differentiate it from the state of Maine's smaller island, Petit Manan.

Grand Manan unexpectedly made international headlines in the summer of 2006 after five local men—Carter Foster, Lloyd Bainbridge, Matthew Lambert, Michael Small and Greg Guthrie, later dubbed the "Grand Manan Five"—decided one drunken night to lay down some vigilante-style whup-ass on the inhabitants of a local crack house. Blows were exchanged, shots were fired and the house was ultimately set on fire. Things then truly took a turn for the weird when the RCMP and firefighters who arrived on the scene were prevented from putting out the blaze by an angry mob that linked arms and chanted "Let it burn! Let it burn!" That's how they take care of business on Grand Manan Island.

Hailed as heroes by some and lawbreakers by others, four of the five vigilantes were later found guilty on weapon possession and arson charges, while the alleged crack dealer will probably never dare set foot on the island again.

KINGDOM FOR A HORSE
SABLE ISLAND, NOVA SCOTIA

Sable Island is technically a part of Nova Scotia and, even though it is considered among its electoral districts, the inclusion is mostly symbolic given that only five of its several hundred permanent residents are actually eligible to vote.

Located around 180 kilometres southeast of Nova Scotia, Sable Island is essentially a long, narrow sand dune that is home to a handful of Environment Canada weather station workers and, weirdly, several hundred wild horses.

There is some mystery surrounding how exactly the horses came to be there. Some think that the chestnut, palamino and black stallions are the descendants of survivors from the island's many, many shipwrecks—over 350 have been recorded—which has given the place the uninviting nickname

"The Graveyard of the Atlantic." (One of the more recent shipwrecks on record could be the famous sword-fishing boat the *Andrea Gail*—the subject of the book, and later the film, *The Perfect Storm*—as Sable Island is where her emergency locator beacon was found washed ashore.)

More than likely, the Sable Island horses are probably descended from horses that were confiscated from the Acadians during the Great Expulsion of 1755 and possibly left on the island by a wealthy Boston ship owner named Thomas Hancock—uncle of *the* John Hancock of super-sized signature fame—who was responsible for transporting many of the Acadians to the United States and may have intended to come back to retrieve the purloined livestock.

In the past, wild horses have been dragged away to become beasts of burden in Cape Breton's coal mines, but since 1960 they've been under federal protection—which is unquestionably a worthier government initiative than the one enacted 60 years ago that saw over 80,000 trees planted on this windswept tip of land in an attempt to stabilize the sandy soil. Not a single one survived.

THE FRENCH CONNECTION
COLLECTIVITÉ TERRITORIALE DE SAINT-PIERRE-ET-MIQUELON

France may have earned itself a reputation for generally surrendering rather than fighting, but you have to give credit where it is due as they have yet to give up on the money-sucking islands of Saint-Pierre and Miquelon.

A bizarre mélange of outport Newfie fishing village and Old World Europe, this unlikely French colony 25 kilometres off Newfoundland's Burin Peninsula is now essentially a footnote to the long, long story of France's forced removal from Canada by the English.

During the 18th century, the islands of Saint-Pierre and Miquelon bounced back and forth between Britain and France no fewer than six times, with all the attendant deportations and repatriations. However, after France lost all its other North American colonies, this wee archipelago—made up of two main islands and a smattering of tiny ones—gained symbolic importance as the last stand of Nouvelle-France and has been securely French since the Treaty of Paris in 1814.

The colony used to be a proverbial jewel in the French crown back in the days when the fishing was good. Until the late 1980s, Saint-Pierre's harbour was usually jammed pack with international fishing boats, and the bars and hotels in town made money hand over fist. A particular boom period was during America's ill-advised Prohibition period (1920–33), when Saint-Pierre became a major player in the booze-smuggling biz and a home away from home for the likes of Al Capone and other gangsters.

Saint-Pierre's raison-d'être came to a crashing halt in 1992 when Canada called a moratorium on cod fishing. Since then, only massive Motherland subsidies—estimated at around $65 million a year—keep the colony afloat.

DID YOU  KNOW?

Saint-Pierre was the setting for the one and only time a guillotine was used in North America, after a man by the name of Joseph Néel was convicted of murder in the late-19th century. The guillotine had to be shipped all the way from Martinique, and then needed to be repaired and sharpened before it could be properly used to lop off the man's head. The sad story inspired the award-winning film *The Widow of Saint-Pierre*, which was shot on location and released in 2000. The guillotine itself now sits in Saint-Pierre's museum.

FRENCH CONNECTION II
MAGDALEN ISLANDS /
ÎLES-DE-LA-MADELEINE, QUÉBEC

Saint-Pierre and Miquleon aren't the only French-speaking islands in Atlantic Canada that aren't technically a part of Atlantic Canada. The Magdalen Islands—also known as "the Maggies" or *les Îles-de-la-Madeleine*—are located in the middle of the Gulf of Saint Lawrence and are much closer to Nova Scotia and PEI than to *la belle province* of Québec.

This wind-swept archipelago was first visited by Mi'kmaq who came to hunt walruses, but it became a popular place for shipwrecked Europeans to become stranded on. Because of its remoteness, it also became a hideout for Acadians trying to escape expulsion during the late-18th century and is still something of a Francophone stronghold, with Acadian flags being flown as frequently as the fleur-de-lis of Québec.

For centuries, the islands were completely cut off by ice during winter, though now there is both an airport and a ferry service to the PEI town of Souris. The archipelago is best known today for being a popular summer vacation spot and a controversial winter seal-clubbing destination.

PRESIDENT'S CHOICE
CAMPOBELLO ISLAND, NEW BRUNSWICK

As of June 1, 2009, Campobello Island is the only place in Canada where residents should probably consider getting a passport even if they don't plan on doing any travelling.

This picturesque island, located at the entrance to Passamaquoddy Bay, is linked to New Brunswick via a ferry during the summer months, but in winter the only way on or off the island is over the Franklin Delano Roosevelt Bridge to neighbouring Lubec, Maine—the easternmost point of the United States. So it's probably not a great place to settle if you've ever had a brush with the law or you're of Arab descent.

The bridge didn't get its name simply due to the American habit of randomly naming pieces of infrastructure after former commanders-in-chief. In fact, Campobello was a long-standing summer retreat for the Roosevelt family and is where FDR was born in 1914. It is also where, at age nine, he fell ill with polio, an illness that resulted in his permanent paralysis from the waist down. Campobello remained a favourite retreat for the prez, and the Roosevelt summer "cottage" (with 34 rooms, really more of a mansion) remained in the family until 1952.

The house is now part of the Roosevelt Campobello International Park, which is the only park in Canada that goes halfsies on its running costs with another country.

DID YOU  KNOW?

The Passamaquoddy Nation originally called the island *Ebaghuit*. After claiming it from the French—who called it the *Port aux Coquilles* (the prosaic "Shell Harbour")—a British captain, possibly angling for a promotion, renamed the island Campobello in 1770 after combining the name of the Governor of Nova Scotia, Lord Campbell, with *bello*, the root word in French, Spanish and Italian meaning "beautiful."

GULF CRISIS
MACHIAS SEAL ISLAND, NEW BRUNSWICK (OR THEN AGAIN, MAYBE MAINE)

This land is your land, this land is my land.

–Woody Guthrie

As far as border disputes go, this one's more than a little bit lame. There is no green line separating warring factions, no submarines dropping flags under the ice, no unfair or unbalanced propaganda on Fox News, and it is highly unlikely any Canadian soldiers will march on Washington to burn down the White House again anytime soon.

Nobody seems entirely sure if Machias Seal Island belongs to Canada or the United States, and for the longest time nobody really cared.

A treeless, uninhabited speck of land south of the Bay of Fundy, the island is stuck in geopolitical limbo due to some ambiguous wording in the Treaty of Paris that states:

> *And that all disputes which might arise in future on the subject of the boundaries of the said United States may be prevented, it is hereby agreed and declared, that the following*

are and shall be their boundaries, from the northwest angle of
Nova Scotia, that angle which is formed by a line drawn due north
from the source of St. Croix River to the highlands....
comprehending all islands within twenty leagues of any part of
the shores of the United States.

Therefore, whether the island is Yankee or Canuck all depends on where precisely in Nova Scotia said imaginary line is drawn from. But in any case, it is Canada who currently maintains the island's lighthouse, the Royal Canadian Mounted Police who police it and the Canadian Wildlife Service who look after the bird sanctuary located there.

The problem of ownership has re-arisen lately because lobsters seem to like the area and lobsters are becoming in short supply these days. Machias Seal Island lies at the centre of a nautical grey zone (or, as they would call it in America, a "gray" zone), a 160-square-kilometre area called Lobster Fishing Area 38B that nobody seems to be in charge of, and so fishermen from both sides of the border have begun taking matters into their own meaty hands.

Recent summers have seen a spat of mangled and tangled gear, heated accusations of vandalism and mutual concerns that overfishing and conflicting regulations will eventually wipe out the crustaceous population for good, which obviously is bad for everyone. It's not as though either country has a spotless track record on this sort of thing—far from it. Canadians are constantly critical of American fisheries laws, the Americans are thoroughly unimpressed by Canadian regulations, and both sides make a valid point.

But at least Machias Seal Island doesn't have oil underneath it. Or seals to club.

BOOM TOWN
BELL ISLAND, NEWFOUNDLAND

Goodness gracious, great balls of fire!

–Jerry Lee Lewis

April 2, 1978, was an uneventful spring Sunday like any other, when out of the blue (literally) there was a high-pitched hum followed by a roaring explosion that was heard over 100 kilometres away. Dozens of witnesses reported seeing a beam of multicoloured light coming straight down from the sky moments before they heard what is now referred to as "The Bell Island Boom."

Two holes, each 0.5 metres deep and almost a full metre wide, were found at the point of impact. Buildings were damaged, chickens were electrocuted, dogs went nuts, power lines melted and more than a few television sets exploded as a result of the strange event.

Within 24 hours, two American representatives from the top secret Los Alamos weapons research facility in New Mexico were on the scene. They promptly declared the baffling boom to be nothing more than "ball lightning" that had been attracted by a nearby abandoned underwater iron mine. They then departed, taking the fried chickens with them.

Unfortunately, nobody is entirely sure what ball lightning *is* exactly. The phenomenon is so weird that for the longest time scientists thought people were simply making it up. Witnesses have reported seeing glowing balls of light—ranging in size from tennis balls to beach balls—that can be either red, white, blue, yellow or green in colour. They've been known to pass harmlessly through walls and windows, and other times violently blast their way through both; they've even been reported floating down the aisles of airplanes while in mid-flight.

Basically, ball lightning is an inexplicable gleaming ball of energy randomly floating through the air. Imagine if Tinkerbell, instead of being an attractive, miniature blonde woman with wings, was a fiery orb that could blast through and/or pass through anything in its path: that's ball lightning.

Probably the best-known example of ball lightning occurred when ill-fated 18th-century Russian physicist Georg Richmann was installing a lightning rod in his St. Petersburg home and was struck in the head by a "pale blue ball of fire." Not only did the mysterious fireball kill him, but it also blew his shoes clean off, knocked his trusty assistant unconscious and blasted a nearby door off its hinges.

Some scientists think that ball lightning is a unique kind of static electricity, or maybe some sort of electrified silicon. Another theory taken quite seriously in certain circles is that ball lightning is caused by "singularities," which is something really huge that doesn't actually take up any space, if you can

wrap your head around that. Or maybe the Greek god Zeus, fed up with the short shrift he's getting worship-wise these days, is simply messing with us.

Filmmakers Jon Whalen and Barbara Doran raised a more sinister explanation for the Bell Island Boom in their 2004 documentary *The Invisible Machine*. They suggest the explosion was triggered by early American military experimentation with electromagnetic pulse weapons (so-called "e-bombs" that can destroy electrical and communications systems, and that may have been used during the "shock and awe" campaign in Iraq) and that these high-energy beams, as they were being focused into the ionosphere, were unexpectedly attracted by the iron in the abandoned mine.

BIZARRE BRIDGES OF ATLANTIC CANADA

ACCURSED TRAVERSE
ANGUS L. MACDONALD BRIDGE, NOVA SCOTIA

Many commuters do a bit of a gut check before driving across this infamous bridge over Halifax Harbour. Two of the three bridges built on the same spot have previously collapsed and, to make matters worse, the third time is supposed to be the charm—or, in this case, the curse.

Legend has it that in the mid-1700s, a British naval ship dropped anchor in the harbour and a young captain named Smith and his crew came ashore to collect drinking water from the Sackville River. While ashore, Smith is said to have spotted a fetching Mi'kmaq lass and fallen in love at first sight. Later that night, the two met again, alone and in secret, and—after some presumably amazing sex—Smith convinced her to sail away with him. (Or maybe he simply kidnapped her; things were done a bit differently back in those days.)

In any case, her father—who happened to be a local chief—was none too pleased to have lost his daughter and he reportedly issued a curse dooming any attempts to span Halifax Harbour, known then as *Chebucto*.

His prophecy stated that the first disaster would occur in a great wind, the second during a great quiet and that the third would cause a great many deaths.

Since then, a railway bridge over the harbour was destroyed in a winter hurricane and its reconstructed replacement collapsed mysteriously in the middle of a calm, sunny day. After a worker fell to his death in the 1950s during the current road bridge's construction, someone in charge had the bright idea to try and find another Mi'kmaq chief to remove the curse. A ceremony was performed that included the literal burying of a hatchet beneath the bridge, but many believe the curse still endures.

COVER STORY
HARTLAND, NEW BRUNSWICK

The world's longest covered bridge didn't start out that way. The 390-metre bridge spanning the Saint John River originally went topless when it was first constructed back in 1901. After undergoing major renovations in 1922, when two spans of the bridge collapsed because of pressure from accumulating river ice, the powers that be decided to put a lid on it.

The decision was quite controversial at the time because town elders were concerned about the corrosive effects this might have on youthful morality. Covered bridges were also called "kissing bridges" because of the darkness and privacy they afforded. Couples crossing these covered bridges in horse-drawn wagons were known to stop halfway across to share a moment or two together, and there was considerable concern as to what might be able to take place within a longer, and much more private, dark tunnel.

Some people believe it brings good luck if you close your eyes, hold your breath and cross your fingers as you drive through a covered bridge. Although doing so will most likely bring the opposite if you're the one driving.

GRILLES IN THE MIST
CANSO CAUSEWAY, NOVA SCOTIA

The 1385-metre-long causeway linking Cape Breton Island to the rest of Canada is the deepest causeway in the world. Over 10 million tonnes of rock were used to fill in the 65-metre deep waters of the Strait of Canso. Part of the Trans-Canada Highway, it also features a single-track railway and a swing bridge over a canal enabling marine traffic to pass through. Construction was completed in 1955 with the final cost to taxpayers tallied at $22 million.

Architecturally impressive as it is, the life of the Canso Causeway hasn't been all accolades and happy commuters, and many people feel the causeway has caused way too many problems. Its presence has not only caused significant environmental damage by altering the tidal patterns of the area, thereby decimating migrating fish populations, but has also allowed many non-native species—the bobcat in particular—to wreak havoc on Cape Breton Island's ecosystem.

BRIDGE OVER TROUBLED LOBSTER
CONFEDERATION BRIDGE, NORTHUMBERLAND STRAIGHT

There's been talk of building a bridge to Prince Edward Island for about as long as the province has been part of Confederation. The world's longest bridge over ice-covered waters is the 13-kilometre Confederation Bridge between Borden, PEI, and Jourimain Island, New Brunswick.

The bridge consists of 44 spans ranging in height from 13 to 40 metres, depending on the depth of water in which they stand. The main girders are 192 metres long, weigh around 7500 tonnes (roughly the heft of two modern battleships) and are built to withstand the force of 3000 tonnes of ice—or about 15 times the force that icebreakers working in the Arctic have to contend with.

The bridge is 11 metres wide and carries two lanes of traffic 24/7, and can be crossed in about 10 minutes if conditions are good. The bridge is gently curved to offset the hypnotic effects of driving in a straight line and a cement barrier blocks drivers from being able to see the water below to prevent the effects of vertigo. The barrier also doubles as a gale shield in a region that is one of the windiest and snowiest in Canada.

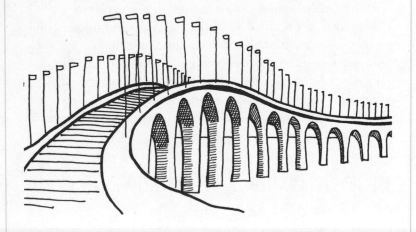

DID YOU KNOW?

Most residents of PEI wanted to name the bridge "Abegweit Crossing," in honour of the original Mi'kmaq name for the island and also for the ferry—the *MV Abegweit*—that the bridge effectively put out of business. They had a strong case, especially considering the province, the so-called "Birthplace of Confederation," already had a Confederation Centre of the Arts, a Confederation Court Mall, a 470-kilometre Confederation Trail and even a ferry named *Confederation* that still plies the waters between PEI and Nova Scotia.

However, seeing as the bridge was finished in the mid-90s right after Québec had nearly succeeded in eschewing the Confederation, the feds opted instead for a name with a bit more nationalistic flair, redundancies aside. Locals generally refer to it simply as "the fixed link."

Weird Natural Wonders of Atlantic Canada

Like most things in Atlantic Canada, the most impressive natural wonders have something to do with the ocean. This is a place where rapids change directions, waves flow upstream, icebergs loom and tides tower.

EXTRA-STRENGTH TIDE
THE BAY OF FUNDY

I think—tide turning—see, as I remember, I was raised in the desert, but tides kind of, it's easy to see a tide turn.

—George W. Bush, on tides

The Bay of Fundy, a body of seawater separating New Brunswick and Nova Scotia, has the highest tides in the world, generally reaching over 15 metres at high tide, or the height of a five-storey building.

The Mi'kmaq believed that the titanic tides in the Bay of Fundy were caused by a giant whale splashing its tail in the water. Oceanographers, for their part, suggest the tides are a coincidence of timing; the 12 hours it takes for a wave to go from the mouth of the bay to the inner shore and back is pretty much the same as the time from one high tide to the next. As the tide comes into the Bay of Fundy, the water level rises between 1.5 and 2.5 metres each hour, bringing in and letting out over 100 billion tonnes of sea water with each cycle— which, to put things in perspective, is roughly the equivalent of the combined 24-hour flow of all the rivers in the world.

The highest water level ever recorded was 21.6 metres and was measured at the head of the Minas Basin during the deadly Saxby Gale of 1869, a perfect storm that was the result of a combination of high winds, an unusually low atmospheric pressure and a spring tide.

The tides also churn up a nutrient-rich smorgasbord that draws up to 15 different species of whales, more than in anywhere else in the world. Local leviathans include humpbacks, finbacks, minkes and even the rare North Atlantic right whale.

The tides also provide power to North America's only tidal power station: the Annapolis Royal Generating Station, an 18-megawatt powerhouse on the Annapolis River that creates enough electricity each day to power 5000 homes and is one of only three tidal power stations on the planet.

WHAT GOES UP MUST COME DOWN
SAINT JOHN, NEW BRUNSWICK

The city of Saint John is famous for its Reversing Falls, an effect created by the ongoing battle between the Bay of Fundy tides and the outflow of the Saint John River. When the tides hit their peak, they crest 4 metres higher than the level of the river and create dangerous rapids that force the current back upstream. When the tide is low, the rapids then flow the other way. While an impressive display of Mother Nature's charms (despite the unfortunate location of the foul-smelling Irving Pulp and Paper Mill next to it), visiting tourists are often disappointed that it is only the river's current that is being reversed and they don't get to see some sort of gravity-defying waterfall.

The Mi'kmaq have a legend about the phenomenon that tells of the giant Glooscap, the keeper of all life. At one point, all the local animals ceded to Glooscap's supremacy except for the beaver, who built a dam across the mouth of what is now the St. John River. Glooscap, unimpressed by the beaver's ingenuity, smashed the dam with his giant club and used the broken pieces to create a series of islands in the river near the falls, as well as the treacherous rapids intended to prevent any new beaver dams from being built. After the Mi'kmaq begged him to change his mind, Glooscap agreed to still the waters for 20 minutes every six hours.

Despite the aforementioned pulp mill, there is currently talk of trying to turn the Falls into more of a tourist attraction by building a new restaurant and installing zip lines so that people can zoom across the gorge attached to harnesses. For now, jet boat tours are available to take tourists through the rapids. There has recently been talk of changing the Falls' name to "The Fundy Vortex" so as not to mislead tourists into expecting to see the fundamental laws of physics suspended.

WHAT A BORE!

PETITCODIAC RIVER, NEW BRUNSWICK
SHUBENACADIE RIVER, NOVA SCOTIA

The Fundy tides also account for one of the world's few examples of a phenomenon known as a "tidal bore." Because the Bay of Fundy is V-shaped, the water literally piles up as it moves up the bay and gets squeezed in by the ever-narrowing sides and the increasingly shallower seabed.

At the very head of the bay, this advancing tide becomes a single wave that varies from just a ripple to more than one metre in height, and it steadily pushes its way up the rivers that empty into the bay, the Petitcodiac and the Shubenacadie being two of the better known.

If the Reversing Falls can be considered a bit of a misnomer, Moncton's Tidal Bore is generally considered anything but. Although the wave that travels up the Petitcodiac River is technically a tidal wave, it won't ever be confused with a tsunami and most viewers find the Bore a bit on the boring side. However, before the Moncton causeway—built in 1968— choked most of the life out of it, the Bore boasted wave heights of 2 metres and was the biggest in North America, able to travel at speeds reaching 14 kilometres an hour.

Although more off the beaten track, the Shubenacadie's Bore still has some kick to it, so much so that local jet boat companies even offer seasonal rides on the twice-daily wave and its attending swirling eddies.

BIG
GARGANTUAN &
RIDICULOUSLY
OVERSIZED

The largest whirlpool in the western hemisphere and one of the five largest in the world, the Old Sow got its name either because of the pig-like sucking noises it makes while churning or, more likely, is a corruption of "sough," an old-school word meaning "a sighing sound." Found in Passamaquoddy Bay just off of Deer Island, the Old Sow ties the record for the world's most powerful whirlpool, with currents measured at 28 kilometres an hour. It has been measured with a diameter of approximately 75 metres.

TIDAL FLOWER
HOPEWELL ROCKS, NEW BRUNSWICK

The famous Fundy tides are also the source of a geological oddity known as "The Flowerpot Rocks." These unusual formations, located not far from Moncton on Hopewell Cape, are islands when the tide is high but reveal themselves to be bizarre-looking, top-heavy spires when the tide is out, able to be explored on foot. As the glaciers retreated after the last ice age, surface water filtered through cracks in the sea-side cliffs and caused the formations to separate from the mainland. For thousands of years since, the tides have carved the base of the rocks at a faster rate than the tops, resulting in their weird shapes.

TRIP OF THE ICEBERGS
ICEBERG ALLEY, NEWFOUNDLAND

I asked for ice, but this is ridiculous.

–John Jacob Astor IV, after finding out the ship he was traveling on, the *RMS Titanic*, had just hit an iceberg

With global warming quickly becoming a global reality, one of the silver linings to this mushroom cloud of doom is that it makes for particularly great iceberg watching. Almost all of the 'bergs in the North Atlantic come from glaciers along the coast of Greenland and nowadays more of them than ever are making it all the way to the east coast of Newfoundland, where they can be ogled in all their frosty tipped glory before they melt.

The term "iceberg alley" was coined to refer to the waters stretching from the northern tip of Labrador to the southern Grand Banks. In 2007, there were five times more icebergs than had ever been seen in a single season. These frozen flotilla tend to be around three storeys high (which, of course, is only

the tip of the iceberg), weigh more than 10 million tonnes and are around 15,000 years old. Most of them calved from glaciers about a year previous and spend several months melting leisurely in arctic bays before passing through the Davis Strait and into the Labrador current that takes them off the Rock.

DID YOU  KNOW?

While most people are content to admire icebergs from a safe distance, some people wondered what they would taste like if combined with triple-distilled grain spirits; keep an eye out for Newfoundland's Iceberg Vodka at a liquor store near you. Using glacier-fresh water harvested from "growlers"—smaller icebergs that have chipped off from larger ones—the St. John's distillery produces this high-end spirit, which came in second only behind the trendier Grey Goose in a blind taste test conducted by experts at the Beverage Tasting Institute.

LITTLE TOUCH OF THE PRAIRIES
TANTRAMAR MARSHES, NEW BRUNSWICK

Skirting the sunbright uplands stretches a riband of meadow,
Shorn of the labouring grass, bulwarked well from the sea

–Charles G.D. Roberts, "Tantramar Revisited"

The Tantramar Marshes near Sackville on the Isthmus of Chignecto are considered to be the world's largest individual hayfield, covering nearly 207 square kilometres. The fertile farming field was reclaimed from the Bay of Fundy's famous tides by an elaborate system of dikes built by Acadian settlers in the late 1600s that still endure today. Hay harvested at Tantramar was in high demand as recently as the 1930s because the salt marsh's soil produced hay that was rich in iodine, which made for high-quality horse fodder in the days before artificial additives.

The noise caused by nesting birds—attracted by the region's extensive freshwater wetlands—inspired the name *tintamarre,* which is French for "ruckus" or "hullabaloo." From August to December, the Tantramar is a stopover for a large number of migrating waterfowl. Two hundred and twenty-eight bird species have been identified at the Amherst Point Migratory Bird Sanctuary: loons, ospreys and numerous species of duck, including pintails, blue-winged teals and green-winged teals, are commonly sighted. The sanctuary is also a breeding site for bald eagles, green herons and snowy egrets. The historic region also inspired the poem "Tantramar Revisited" by Charles G.D. Roberts, which is a poetic staple in Canadian Lit 101 classes across the country.

MAGNETIC EAST
MAGNETIC HILL, NEW BRUNSWICK

This Atlantic Canada tourist destination has, by far, the greatest drawing power of them all and is located on the outskirts of the city of Moncton. The attraction of Magnetic Hill is actually based on an optical illusion: if you drive your car to the bottom of the hill, put it in neutral and take your foot off the brake, the car appears to coast uphill. Having once visited Magnetic Hill with a car full of guys when I was a teenager, I can attest to the fact that the illusion also works if, once you've coasted to the top, you then get out and strain to push the car back "down" the hill.

The allure of Magnetic Hill is caused by a simple trick of the eye: from atop the hill the level of the horizon is hidden and the trees grow at an angle instead of straight up.

Despite this mundane explanation, Magnetic Hill still manages to pull people in. It was the setting for the Atlantic Canada's largest concert—a 2005 outdoor show by the Rolling Stones that attracted an estimated 75,000 people—and, before that, was the site of the largest gathering in East Coast history when Pope John Paul II came to town in 1984.

BIG
GARGANTUAN &
RIDICULOUSLY
OVERSIZED

The biggest mountain in Atlantic Canada and the highest peak east of the Rockies is the 1652-metre-high Mount Caubvick. Found way, way up north in the Torngat Mountains, this lofty peak straddles the tip of the border with Québec. Although it has a relatively low elevation, Mount Caubvick rises steeply from near sea level and features glaciers, steep cirques and craggy ridges. The Innu believe that the spirit world and the world of the living overlap in these mountains; in Inuktitut, the word torngat translates as "home of the spirits." The bleak, mostly treeless landscape is primarily inhabited by caribou and black bears, and the closest human settlement is the rarely bustling Kangiqsualujjuaq (population 600 or so), some 150 kilometres away.

Saddled with the rather unimaginative moniker L1 for decades—L for Labrador and 1 for being the highest—the mountain was re-christened in 1981 to honour the memory

BIG
GARGANTUAN &
RIDICULOUSLY
OVERSIZED

of one of the five Inuit who went to England with explorer George Cartwright in 1772. Caubvick was the only one to see his home again after all his companions died overseas from smallpox. Although the mountain's summit rests entirely within Labrador, Mount Caubvick is also considered to be the largest mountain in the province of Québec, where it is known as Mont d'Iberville. Québec, being Québec, insisted on giving the mountain their own name in honour of Pierre Le Moyne, Sieur d'Iberville (1661–1706), a French soldier famous for sinking several English ships and burning to the ground dozens of English settlements throughout Atlantic Canada.

Weird Creatures Great and Small

These days, the animal most people around the world associate with Atlantic Canada is, unfortunately, the harp seal. Or, to be more specific, the baby harp seal.

Clubbing baby seals to death for their pelts, a centuries-old winter tradition on the ice floes off the coast of Newfoundland, is largely deplored internationally nowadays, and its controversial continued existence thanks to subsidies by the Canadian government essentially means that thousands of dollars are brought into the local economy at the cost of millions of dollars lost because of boycotts of Canadian exports. The controversial annual hunt is considered to be the largest slaughter of marine mammals in the world.

The reason for the continued seal hunt is largely due to the lack of cod fish, which used to be the creature most people associated with Atlantic Canada and which were once so bountiful that pretty much all you had to do was cast a net over the side of your boat and you could bring up dozens of fish—it was what brought the Europeans to the region in the first place. Since the collapse of the fisheries industry, however, seal hunting has returned mainly as a make-work project for otherwise out-of-work fishermen.

All of which is unfortunate, given that there are plenty of other members of the animal kingdom in Atlantic Canada worth looking at, some mythical, others just weird.

ATTACK OF THE 50-FOOT WOMAN
BAIE-DES-CHALEURS, NEW BRUNSWICK

The first European to report some sort of weird creature in North America was none other than famed French explorer Samuel de Champlain, which is rather fitting given that he later had a mysterious monster of his own named after him, Lake Champlain's "Champ." After making his second voyage into the Gulf of Saint Lawrence in the early 1600s, Champlain gave the following description of a sea monster that had his Mi'kmaq guides shaking in their moccasins:

> *Near the Bay of Chaleurs, towards the south, there is an island where a terrible monster resides, which the savages call Gougou, and which they told me had the form of a woman, though very frightful, and of such a size that they told me the tops of the masts of our vessel would not reach to her middle, so great do they picture her; and they say that she has often devoured and still continues to devour many savages; these she puts, when she can catch them, into a great pocket, and afterwards eats them...*
> (*Voyages Of Samuel de Champlain*)

When not terrorizing unfortunate seafarers, the Gougou is said to spend her time lurking in an undersea cave making loud hissing noises and generally being horrifying. Captain Prevert, one of Champlain's men, also reported hearing strange hissing sounds when he sailed past her supposed lair, though it's possible that he was simply trying to humour his boss.

Although it has been many centuries since the last reported sighting of the Gougou, this can perhaps be explained by her penchant for devouring all potential witnesses and the possibility that some sailors who were thought to have been drowned at sea actually met a different end entirely. If she is out there, I'd like to think she looks a lot like Ursula the sea witch from the classic Disney film *The Little Mermaid*.

It's worth mentioning that some nay-saying etymologists believe there is no such thing as a giant evil hag living underwater off the coast of New Brunswick and that the legend is most likely related to earthquakes, given that "Gougou" sounds very much like *kukwes*, the Mi'kmaq word for seismic tremors.

SMALL, MINISCULE AND RIDICULOUSLY UNDERSIZED
THE LEGEND OF THE NAGUMWASUCK

The Nagumwasuck are the fairy-like guardian spirits of the Passamaquoddy Nation, and they live a smaller-scale lifestyle much like the tribe's traditional one. Although I've never seen one myself, they're described as being around 20 centimetres tall, extremely thin and ugly, with pointy noses and deep-set eyes. They are said to enjoy helping humans whenever they can but don't like to be seen by people because of their hideous appearance, which, obviously, is why very few people have ever seen one.

According to native mythology, the Nagumwasuck once ranged throughout southern Atlantic Canada, but are now confined to a handful of Indian reserves. They are said to currently suffer from a deep depression brought about by the encroachment of their lands and, unable to apply for financial compensation from the government for their losses, they spend their days singing mournful dirges and talking about the good old days with the comparatively giant human tribal elders.

LOCH STALKING PERILS

LAKE UTOPIA, NEW BRUNSWICK
CRESCENT LAKE, NEWFOUNDLAND

No country in the world has more lakes said to have mysterious monsters lurking in them than Canada. Mind you, Canada has roughly *two million* lakes to choose from, so perhaps this is to be expected.

The most famous is the oft-sighted Ogopogo of British Columbia's Lake Okanagan, but a cryptozoologist's "who's who" list of lake monsters also includes the likes of Manitoba's knockoffs Manipogo and Winipogo—also plying the 'pogo shtick in the waters of Lake Manitoba and Lake Winnipeg— the aforementioned Champ of Lake Champlain, the Lake Erie Monster, Kempenfelt Kelly (or Beaverton Bessie) of Ontario's Lake Simcoe and Memphre of Quebec's Lac Memphremagog.

In Atlantic Canada, the most famous are New Brunswick's Lake Utopia Monster ("Old Ned" to friends) and Crescent Lake's Cressie in Newfoundland.

A place named "Utopia" might not be where you'd expect to find a monster dwelling in its depths, but the lake was named with tongue firmly in cheek when newly arrived Loyalists were none too impressed to discover the land they'd been promised was actually located underwater.

Sightings of an enormous eel-like creature, approximately 12 to 15 metres long, in Lake Utopia go back centuries and predate the arrival of Europeans. The Maliseet tell an early tale of two canoeists who were chased across the lake by an angry giant serpent but, apart from a mid-1800s report of the creature busting though the ice in an attempt to feast on an ice fisherman, most reports are of a relatively benign creature that simply likes to bask in the sun. The most recent reported sighting was in 1996 by local retirees Roger and Lois Wilcox, who were also out canoeing at the time.

Lake Utopia is around 7 kilometres long and only 3 kilometres at its widest, which hardly seem like Utopian confines for a sizable serpent. However, the lake is connected to the Magaguadavic River and, from there, to the Atlantic Ocean by one of the deepest natural canals in the world.

One theory that may have some legs to it is that the monster (or generations of monsters) is actually a species of giant eel, since eels spawn at sea but always return to their native lake, a bit like salmon only in reverse. Seasonal spawning patterns could also explain why Old Ned sightings are always a few years apart and why a similar creature has been spotted in the nearby waters of Passamaquoddy Bay.

Although the Magaguadavic (a Maliseet word meaning, interestingly, "river of big eels") passes through a waterfall and a hydroelectric station in the town of St. George on its way to the sea, it is a well-known fact there are a series of underwater tunnels beneath the town that could conceivably be used by a savvy sea monster to return home.

The premise that lake monsters are actually sea monsters that travel through subterranean passages has also been floated to explain the existence of the most famous of them all: Scotland's Loch Ness Monster. Both lakes share a proximity to the ocean and both lie between the 45th and 50th parallels—a circle of latitude that forms a beltway of lake monster sightings around the globe, which also happens to include northern Newfoundland's Crescent Lake.

The Beothuk people knew the Crescent Lake creature as *woodum haoot* ("pond demon") or *haoot tuwedyee* ("swimming demon"). The first white person to report seeing a serpent swimming in Crescent Lake was an early resident of the lake-side community of Robert's Arm who was out picking berries in the early 1900s. Fifty years later, two local men who may or may not have been drinking at the time reported seeing an overturned rowboat that, as they approached, suddenly became a giant slippery mass before sinking beneath the waves. An

otherwise inexplicable huge hole in the lake's ice was reported in the winter of 1981. A few years later, scuba divers attempted to recover the body of a pilot who crashed in the lake and they claim to have been forced to turn back after being chased off by a school of giant eels.

The most recent sighting came in 2003 when local resident Vivian Short claimed to have seen Cressie while out driving with a friend. As she explained it to CBC News: "I was just a screamin', 'We saw Cressie, we saw Cressie!' Excited, eh... Well, I said to my friend, 'Oh my, that's big. That could eat four or five people if they were swimming.'"

DID YOU KNOW?

Old Ned isn't Lake Utopia's only unexplained mystery. In 1863, a local stonemason searching for brick material came across a strange rock medallion that bore a carving of a man's face. There are various theories to explain it: it is an ancient carving by indigenous people (despite neither the Mi'kmaq or Maliseet nations having any history of stone carving); it is a portrait carved by an artist who traveled with Samuel de Champlain in the early 1600s; it is proof positive that ancient Egyptian explorers made it to North America's shores; or it could simply be a prank. The mysterious medallion is currently on display at the New Brunswick Museum in Saint John.

BIG

GARGANTUAN & RIDICULOUSLY OVERSIZED

Sussex, New Brunswick

When I was a kid, one of the highlights of a drive through Sussex was seeing the giant cow that stood in a field by the side of the highway. One day I was surprised to see an equally over sized calf standing beside her and so made the only logical conclusion: that the hefty heifer must have been knocked up by a gigantic bull that presumably wanders the countryside of southern New Brunswick in search of potential mates.

Turns out I was mistaken; instead, the 4-metre tall cow and her offspring are cement statues erected to draw attention to Sussex's status as the "Dairy Centre of the Maritimes" by New Brunswick's ubiquitous Irving family. The humongous Holsteins were built by Harold MacEachern, who was also behind the similarly massive moose found in the Newfoundland communities of Goobies and Deer Lake.

GREAT WHITE EAST

You're gonna need a bigger boat.

–Police Chief Brody, *Jaws*

If you ever saw the movie *Jaws*, you no doubt remember the scene when a young Richard Dreyfuss went inside an underwater cage to get a closer look at the titular man-eating shark. If you thought this looked like fun, even after the man-eating shark destroyed the cage and nearly made a meal of him, then Nova Scotia's Lunenburg Ocean Adventures might have just the trip for you!

From late August to October, certified scuba divers can sign up to be lowered in a special cage in the hope of encountering a shark (not to mention whales, blue fin tuna, seals, dolphins and sea turtles) up close and personal.

The owners say on their website that seeing a blue shark is the most common but "the occasional mako is always a surprise." Before signing on the dotted line, thrill seekers may want to pause and consider that a truly enormous great white shark (*Carcharodon carcharias*) was caught in waters not too far away—not that there has ever been a recorded fatal shark attack in Atlantic Canada's waters.

In August 2004, skipper Jamie Doucette and his crew took part in the annual Yarmouth Shark Scramble fishing derby and landed one of the biggest great whites ever. After they hooked the beast, the shark fought for about 15 minutes before finally surfacing to take a look at its tormentors, long enough for a crewmember to get a rope around its tail. The shark then took off, towing the 13-metre fishing boat sideways and backward through the water at speeds estimated at around seven knots. If this sounds familiar, it's because it too was like a scene straight out of *Jaws*, only one with a happier ending, at least for the fishermen.

The shark eventually drowned and the fishermen made it back to shore safely. The prize-winning catch was measured as a whopping 3.3 metres long and weighed 492 kilograms.

As big a fish as it was, this particular great white pales in comparison to one that was discovered in 1930 trapped in a herring weir near Grand Manan, New Brunswick, which at 11.3 metres long and weighing 2500 kilograms, is listed in the *Guinness Book of World Records* as the largest ever caught. However, many marine biologists think this is too impossibly large to be an actual great white and suggest that instead it was only a harmless basking shark. In any case: *Caveat emptor* (Buyer beware!).

BIG
GARGANTUAN & RIDICULOUSLY OVERSIZED

Goobies, Newfoundland

The village of Goobies is little more than a gas stop on the Trans-Canada Highway whose most recognizable feature is a giant concrete moose named Morris standing outside the local Irving station. (For the record, Morris isn't the only concrete moose to be found standing outside a Newfoundland Irving station—Deer Lake has one as well.) This is perhaps fitting given that, besides stopping for coffee or gas, the only other reason people stop in Goobies is to report a collision with an actual moose. They say there are as many moose in Newfoundland as there are people, possibly because the moose has yet to figure out how move to Alberta to look for work.

What's weird about all these moose is that there wasn't a single one on the island until 1904, when four exceptionally fertile moose were set loose after being brought over from New Brunswick. Although moose hunting is a popular pastime in Newfoundland, the ungainly ungulates are considered by many people to be nothing more than an unnecessarily imported road hazard—more than 700 moose-related collisions, often fatal, occur in the province each year. The problem is that most drivers won't hit a moose but rather will get hit *by* a moose. The largest member of the deer family, a moose can stand over 2 metres tall and males can weigh between 400 to 550 kilograms.

When a car collides with a moose, it usually only sideswipes the creature's legs, causing the rest of the moose to crash down on top of the car and its passengers. To

☞

BIG
GARGANTUAN &
RIDICULOUSLY
OVERSIZED

make matters worse, moose tend to convene near roadways to feed on the roadside vegetation as well as to get away from flies in summer and deep snow in winter. They're none too bright either— when panicked by an approaching vehicle, they're just as likely to run in front of it to escape as run away from it.

CANADIAN KRAKEN
THIMBLE TICKLE BAY, NEWFOUNDLAND

Holy smoke! What a scuffle! All hands are excited
'Tis a wonder to me that there's nobody drowned.
There's a bustle, confusion, a wonderful hustle
They're all jiggin' squid on the squid-jiggin' ground.

–Arthur Scammell, from the Newfoundland folk classic,
"Squid-Jiggin' Ground"

For centuries, sailors from across the seven seas have told stories of monsters with multiple arms that could reach as high as a ship's mainmast and sink even the sturdiest of vessels. Artwork from ancient Greece depict what appear to be giant squids attacking their fishing boats; antique Japanese woodcuts show similar creatures locked in combat with whales; and Viking legends tell of the frightful Kraken, a multi-armed, multi-headed monster so large it was often (and quite fatally) mistaken by sailors for land. Aristole and Pliny the Elder both wrote of deadly giant squids, as did novelists Herman Melville and Jules Verne centuries later. You might remember the creatures from such films as *The Beast* and *Pirates of the Caribbean: Dead Man's Chest*.

There seemed to be plenty of evidence suggesting the existence of some sort of species of super-sized squid out there, but for the longest time there wasn't any scientific proof to back it up. Then in 1861, the French gunboat *Alecton* encountered a giant squid near the Canary Islands and managed to harpoon it, killing it after a long struggle.

Unfortunately when they tried to drag their oversized prize back on board, the rope snapped and most of the monster fell back into the water and sank. Only one huge tentacle survived, but it was enough to prove the legend wasn't just a tall tale.

Strangely, throughout the 1870s, dozens of giant squids began suddenly washing up on the shores of Newfoundland—and nobody has any idea why. (Personally I'd like to think it was some sort of ill-advised attempt at a land assault to avenge their smaller squid cousins that Newfoundlanders harvest commercially. But I digress.)

Stranger still, similar creatures also began showing up on the other side of the world on the shores of New Zealand in what became known as a banner decade for giant squid groundings. Maybe it had something to do with some sort of fatal attraction to large islands that begin with the word "new."

All of the beached giant squid were quite dead by the time they were discovered except the largest of them all—which remains the largest ever officially recorded—a monster that was still alive and flailing when three fishermen from Glover's Harbour,

Newfoundland, came across it near Thimble Tickle Bay on November 2, 1878. The men managed to hook the dying beast, which had ran aground in the shallow waters of an ebb tide, with a grapnel and then tied it to a tree to keep it from washing back out to sea.

The beast's torpedo-shaped body was measured as being nearly 7 metres long, with 11-metre tentacles covered in 40-centimetre wide suckers, and was estimated to weigh around 2 metric tonnes. The miraculous scientific discovery was then promptly chopped up into dog food.

The Atlantic giant squid (*Architeuthis dux*) is hands down one of the scariest looking creatures out there. These carnivorous mollusks have eight arms covered in razor-sharp suckers, two specially designed tentacles to draw prey into their gaping maws, three hearts and even a beak; they also have the ability to change their skin color to blend into their surroundings and can release black ink in order to blind and confuse their prey. Their huge, unnerving eyes—bigger than a human head—are the largest of any animal living or extinct, and they can lurk at depths in which the water pressure is enough to a crush a modern nuclear submarine. Even Chuck Norris wouldn't want to mess with one.

Newfoundland is also one of the few known places in the world where people have survived a giant squid attack. Five years previous to the discovery of the Thimble Tickle squid, three fishermen in Conception Bay—Daniel Squires, Theophilus Piccot and 12-year-old Tom Piccot—rowed their dory over to a mysterious floating mound and made the mistake of poking it with a hook. The startled giant squid consequently attacked, wrapping a tentacle around their vessel and drawing the terrified trio toward its waiting jaws. Fortunately, young Tom managed to get his hands on a handy hatchet and was able to sever one of its arms, causing the squid to release their boat and retreat. The fishermen managed to make it back to shore with the severed arm still clinging to their dory, which was measured at 5.8 metres long (the severed arm, that is, not the dory).

While the Thimble Tickle squid is the largest on record—since commemorated with a 17-metre long statue in Glover Harbour—there are doubtlessly much bigger ones currently roaming the oceans. Fifty-centimeter sucker scars found on whale carcasses suggest some could be as large as 36 metres long, though this is inconclusive because the scars would grow at the same time as the whale does. But sperm whales are the giant squid's only known predator, which is all the more amazing given that the squids are often the same length as a whale (if only a fraction of their weight).

DID YOU  KNOW?

In fact, there could very well be *much* bigger giant squids out there. In the summer of 1997, the National Oceanic and Atmospheric Administration recorded a freakishly loud sound in the ocean, so loud that two microphones over 5000 kilometres apart recorded the same noise. The sound—dubbed "The Bloop"—doesn't sound like much when played at normal speed, but fortunately the NOAA did us weirdness enthusiasts the favour of speeding up the recording to 16 times the normal speed, creating an audible "Bloop!" Hear it for yourself at www.pmel.noaa.gov/vents/acoustics/sounds/bloop.html.

Scientists have determined that the mysterious sound wave's pattern indicates it was made by an animal, but there is no known creature even remotely big enough to generate that kind of noise.

CONSIDER THE GLOBSTER
FORTUNE BAY, NEWFOUNDLAND
PARKER'S COVE, NOVA SCOTIA

Giant squid are not the only bizarre carcasses to wash up on the shores of Atlantic Canada. Weird creatures have been showing up unexpectedly for as long as anyone can remember, but in the early-21st century we have seen a peculiar boom of blobs. The first to make headlines was the so-called "Newfoundland Blob," a pile of fishy-smelling goo nearly 6 metres long that washed ashore near the Newfoundland fishing village of St. Bernard's on Fortune Bay in August 2001. It immediately caused international buzz that some sort of sea monster had finally been discovered.

Unidentified blobs, also know as "globsters" (a term coined by Ivan T. Sanderson to describe an equally mysterious find in Tasmania back in 1960), have long been a cryptozoological curiosity as they are obviously made of flesh but have decayed so badly that they often lack bones or any real distinguishing features.

Unfortunately for the Mulders of the world, Scully was right on this one. After scientists from St. John's Memorial University performed DNA analysis of the unidentified mass, it was determined to be nothing more interesting than the rotted-out carcass of a sperm whale.

But then, the very next year, yet another weird carcass washed up in Parker's Cove on the Bay of Fundy. The 8-metre long body had a small head with a long thin neck attached to a massive body of cavities and cartilage. Stranger still, long strands of coarse hair covered the creature's fins.

Paranormal researchers were quick to tell anyone who would listen that it was definitely the body of a sea monster, or just a regular monster that drowned, or anything paranormal. Possibly they were just happy someone was talking to them.

But once again, truth turned out to be lamer than fiction. After it too underwent DNA analysis, it was determined to be the remains of a basking shark. Basking sharks are gentle filter feeders, like whales. Largely made of cartilage, they decompose in a way that leaves them looking like a veritable sea monster, and their blubber becomes stringy as it decomposes, closely resembling fur.

BIG GARGANTUAN & RIDICULOUSLY OVERSIZED

Stewiacke, Nova Scotia

This small town in southern Colchester County claims to have the world's largest statue of a mastodon. The mammoth statue was erected to commemorate the discovery of skeletal remains found in a local quarry. ☞

BIG
GARGANTUAN &
RIDICULOUSLY
OVERSIZED

Often confused with wooly mammoths, American mastodons (*Mammut americanum*) were similar in height—roughly 3 metres tall at the shoulder—but much stockier, with wider heads and smaller teeth more suited to chewing leaves than grazing trees. The name "mastodon" refers to the creature's mastoid teeth, which is Greek for "nipple teeth."

Mastodons first appeared on the scene about four million years ago and died out only 10,000 years ago. They were an important food source for prehistoric humans, and experts are still trying to determine what role, if any, our ancestors played in their extinction.

Erected in 1994, Stewiacke's mastodon is made of fiberglass and steel, stands 4.5 metres tall, is 7.5 metres long and weighs in at a whopping 1400 kilograms, which is considerably larger than the replica wooly mammoth found in Kyle, Saskatchewan, which was built for similar reasons.

THE CELEBRATED THUMPING FROG OF YORK COUNTY
FREDERICTON, NEW BRUNSWICK

Jeremiah was a bullfrog,
Was good friend of mine.
I never understood a single word he said
But I helped him drink his wine.

–Three Dog Night, "Jeremiah Was A Bullfrog"

Above and beyond the most famous amphibian in Atlantic Canada—after Kermit the Frog of course—is a super-sized specimen known as the Coleman Frog.

The story goes that a unique friendship was forged between the freakish frog and a local hotel proprietor named Fred Coleman after they met on Killarney Lake in the late 1800s. Coleman started bringing his new pal buttermilk, whisky and whey whenever he went fishing in the lake, and this atypical amphibian diet is said to have caused the already massive frog to pack on even more weight, eventually tipping the scales at an unprecedented 19 kilograms.

Alas, one dark summer day in 1885 some frustrated fishermen supposedly used dynamite to flush out some fish and inadvertently caused the giant frog to croak. Coleman is said to have been inconsolable and, as a memorial to their enduring friendship (or possibly as a means to attract guests to his Barker House hotel), he had the deceased frog stuffed and placed prominently inside his saloon.

There it sat for years, where it also doubled as popular place for patrons to stub out their cigars. After being rediscovered in the attic of one of Coleman's descendants in the 1950s, the Coleman Frog was given a new home at Fredericton's York Sunbury Museum, where it is currently the museum's star attraction.

While it's true that visitors occasionally comment on how the giant frog, which is kept behind glass, looks more like an amateurish papier-mâché model, and some skeptics have even gone so far as to suggest that it bears an uncanny resemblance to a frog featured in an old ad campaign for a cough medicine guaranteed to relieve "the frog in your throat," the museum's staff insists there's no bull regarding the frog and that the bullfrog's tale is no shaggy dog story. DNA testing has been suggested but, in the end, the decision was made to let sleeping frogs lie.

A SHAGGY DOG TALE
NEWFOUNDLAND'S NEWFOUNDLAND

Beauty without vanity, strength without insolence, courage without ferocity, and all the virtues of man without his vices.

–Lord Byron's inscription on the gravestone
of his pet Newfoundland, Boatswain

To the majority of people outside Canada, the word "Newfoundland" more often refers to a type of massive shaggy dog with a penchant for rescuing people rather than an isolated island in the Atlantic.

Nobody is entirely sure about the origins of this distinctive dog. The best guess is that the dog is a cross between an indigenous breed kept by aboriginals and the giant mastiffs brought over by Portuguese fishermen in the 1400s. By the time Newfoundland was established as a colony in the early 1600s, the Newfoundland dog was already well established. Classified as a working dog in the "giant" weight range, this good-natured beast generally weighs between 45 and 70 kilograms—though the largest ever recorded, named Bonzo Bear, tipped the scales at 120 kilograms, measured over 2 metres from nose to tail and once dragged a nearly 2000-kilogram weight a total distance of 4.6 metres, according to the *Guinness Book of World Records.*

As much at home at sea as they are on land, "Newfs" are the only dogs in the world that not only have webbed feet but also eschew the traditional "dog paddle" in favour of the breast-stroke. They also have thick, water-resistant coats and enormous lungs, enabling them to swim for hours at a time. Newfoundlands were considered prized assets for fishermen, capable of hauling fishing nets to and from boats as well as being natural-born lifeguards, a bit like black, waterlogged versions of Saint Bernards, though without the miniature keg of whiskey on their collars.

There are countless stories of Newfoundlands carrying lifelines to sinking ships or jumping into the sea if someone was washed overboard. (Strange as it may seem, few fishermen knew how to swim in the olden days.) One of the most famous rescues occurred one winter night in 1919 off the coast of (appropriately enough) Newfoundland itself when a steamship capsized during a blizzard and a dog named Tang towed it to shore, saving the lives of all 92 people on board. For his valiant efforts, Tang was later awarded a gold medal from the famous insurance company Lloyds of London, which he wore on his collar for the rest of his life.

DID YOU KNOW?

Less dramatic but more historically significant, an unnamed Newfoundland also saved the life of Napoleon Bonaparte in 1815 when he was washed overboard during his famous escape from exile on the island of Elba.

BIG
GARGANTUAN &
RIDICULOUSLY
OVERSIZED

**Campbellton,
New Brunswick**

This northern New Brunswick city is located on the banks of the Restigouche River, considered to be one of the finest Atlantic salmon fishing rivers in North America. The city celebrates its main meal ticket with both an annual salmon festival and an impressive steel sculpture known as Restigouche Sam. Made of roughly 2000 stainless steel scales welded onto a tubular frame by artist William Kisman, the one-tonne sculpture is 8.5 metres tall and is surrounded by a fountain to give the appearance that Sam is leaping into mid-air, as real-life salmon are wont to do.

CRUSTACEAN NATION
SHEDIAC, NEW BRUNSWICK

What has no brain, two pincers, five pairs of legs, teeth in its stomach, comes in a variety of different colours and can emit a menacing growl? Answer: the delicious American lobster (*Homarus americanus*).

People from Atlantic Canada love to tell newcomers how back in the olden days the children of fishermen had to "get by" on

WEIRD CREATURES GREAT AND SMALL

lobster sandwiches for their school lunches, while the rich kids got to dine on more refined delicacies like peanut butter and jelly. It took a lot longer than you might think for people to realize that these copious crustaceans were actually quite tasty, particularly when served with melted butter.

It's strange to think that early European settlers in Atlantic Canada were often close to starving to death with such an abundant supply of lobster nearby—maybe it had something to do with them being so damn ugly. (The lobsters, not the settlers.) Or maybe it was because of one of the more bizarre passages in the Bible that states: *They [shellfish] shall be an abomination to you; you shall not eat their flesh, but you shall regard their carcasses as an abomination. Whatever in the water does not have fins or scales; that shall be an abomination to you."* (Leviticus 11:11–12)

Your guess is as good as mine as to what God is supposed to have had against one of His more mouth-watering creations— probably something to do with mysterious ways and what not. Regardless, the social status of lobster changed dramatically in the late 1800s when they were made trendy by America's famous Rockefeller family, who used to spend their summers in nearby Bar Harbor and helped turn their newfound Maine course meal into a status symbol for the rich.

Nowadays lobsters are huge in Atlantic Canada, both figuratively and literally. According to the *Guinness Book of World Records*, the largest lobster ever landed—weighing 20.15 kilograms and measuring just over one metre long—was pulled from Nova Scotian waters in 1977.

Meanwhile, a beach town named Shediac along the Northumberland Strait is the self-proclaimed "Lobster Capital of the World."

To lend credence to their crustacean claim, this town—a half hour drive from the city of Moncton—not only holds a famous

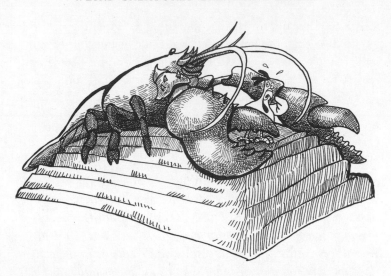

lobster festival each July that draws around 50,000 tourists but has also erected an 11-metre wide, 50-tonne cast-iron lobster that stands poised to make a meal of anyone standing in front of it. Sculptor Winston Bronnum spent three years completing the project, estimated to be worth around $180,000, which now attracts around 500,000 people a year to Shediac to have their picture taken with it.

While Shediac's lobster is indisputably the biggest of its kind, it's worth noting that it's not the only enormous tribute in Atlantic Canada that pays homage to the *homard*. The Pettipas Market in Auld's Cove outside of Antingonish, Nova Scotia, has both an enormous blue papier-mâché lobster and a red one made out of an old metal navigational buoy.

Although commercial fishermen use cages to catch lobster, it is quite easy (though highly illegal) to simply grab one while, say, out snorkeling. Far be it for me to recommend breaking federal fisheries laws, but there is a popular local legend that offers a potential way out of being caught red-handed.

The story goes that a man (invariably a Newfie but, for the sake of political correctness, we'll pretend that he could be from anywhere in Atlantic Canada) was walking up a wharf one day carrying a lobster in each hand when a Fisheries Officer stopped him. As the officer began writing him a ticket, the man hastily explained that the lobsters were, in fact, trained pets.

"Each day I take these two down to the wharf and put them in the water for a swim. While they swim, I sit on the wharf and have a smoke. After about 15 minutes I whistle and up come my two lobsters, and I take them home again," he explained.

Not believing him, the Fisheries Officer insisted on a demonstration. Down they went to the end of the wharf and the man gently lowered the lobsters into the water. After about 15 minutes, the Fisheries Officer suggested it was probably about time to start whistling.

"What for?" the man replied.

"To call in the lobsters."

"What lobsters?" he asked.

Dorchester, New Brunswick

This tiny town, located on the mouth of the Memramcook River, is best known as the home of the Dorchester Penitentiary, an infamous hoosegow that was once home for wrongfully convicted inmates Donald Marshall and David Milgaard. But it's also home to an enormous statue of a semipalmated sandpiper (*Calidris pusilla*), a bird not otherwise known for its gigantic stature, which is located in front of the town hall.

☞

 **BIG GARGANTUAN & RIDICULOUSLY OVERSIZED** The statue was built to commemorate the annual Sandpiper Festival held each July, the time of year when the miniature birds stop by on their migration between the Arctic and South America. Semipalmated sandpipers are the most common sandpipers in Atlantic Canada and flocks of more than 200,000 have been recorded in nearby Shepody Bay during their yearly exodus.

Semipalmated sandpipers can be considered to be a bit on the weird side for a couple of reasons. For starters, the chicks aren't fed by their parents; instead, they hatch with their eyes open and with adult-sized legs (mind you, the adults are only around 14 centimetres tall and weigh a mere 30 grams or so) and immediately start searching for insects to eat.

And though Dorchester's mudflats are famous for being a key stopover habitat for these sandpipers, the birds have also been known to fly non-stop on their migration to south of the equator, a distance of over 3000 kilometres. Ornithologists remain at a loss to explain how such tiny birds are able to accomplish this.

NUTHIN' BUT PUFFINS
WITLESS BAY ECOLOGICAL RESERVE, NEWFOUNDLAND

The northern hemisphere's answer to the penguin, the Atlantic puffin (*Fratercula arctica*) is yet another bird whose very existence suggests that God must have a sense of humour. About the size of a pigeon, with black and white tuxedo plumage, a distinctive striped beak and orange feet, it is known as both the "clown of the sea" and the "sea parrot." Although occasionally mistaken for a penguin, the puffin is often recognizable to non-bird lovers because of its frequent appearance in cutesy "No Puffin" signs meant to politely discourage people from smoking in public.

The puffin is the official bird of Newfoundland and Labrador, and almost all of North America's puffins breed around the province's coastlines, particularly at the Witless Bay Ecological Reserve near St. John's, where an estimated 260,000 nest under the Witless protection program during the late spring and summer. Nobody seems quite sure how "Witless Bay" earned its name, but I'd like to think it is somehow connected to whoever named the main island of the world's largest puffin colony "Gull Island."

The puffin is truly a remarkable little bird. For starters, it doesn't build its nest in a tree but instead digs a burrow. It can beat its wings around 400 times a minute, so fast that they become a blur and make an airborne puffin look a bit like a black and white football. A pelagic bird that feeds by diving for fish, the puffin is far better at swimming than it is at flying and can spend several years at sea, able to sleep on the water, before returning to land to breed.

DID YOU KNOW?

The puffin unexpectedly found itself at the centre of a political controversy in late 2008. Liberal deputy leader Michael Ignatieff had recently waxed poetical about the puffin while on the campaign trail in Newfoundland, calling it a "noble bird" that somehow exemplified Liberal values. The Conservative Party seized upon this supposed misstep and, in a bizarre attempt to appeal to younger voters, built a website that featured a puffin pooping on the shoulder of then-Liberal leader Stéphane Dion. After a lot of outraged huffing and puffing, Prime Minister

Stephen Harper was subsequently forced to publicly apologize for what inevitably came to be called "Puffingate."

THE RAW DEAL
BALLANTYNE'S COVE, NOVA SCOTIA

On the surface it might seem like Atlantic Canada's biggest attraction for the Japanese would be Prince Edward Island, given that so many Japanese tourists swarm the island each summer to gobble up any paraphernalia to do with that little orphan Anne of Green Gables. A lesser known local connection to the land of the rising sun is found in Ballantyne's Cove, a sleepy fishing village located on the Northumberland Shore.

Every fall from September to November, hundreds of fishing boats set out to sea in search of bluefin tuna (*Thunnus thynnus*). Larger ones weigh around 275 kilograms and can garner thousands of dollars apiece from buyers because one of the biggest delicacies in the sushi biz, toro sashimi, is made from the fat of bluefins and Ballantyne's Cove is one of its main suppliers.

Unfortunately, Ballantyne's Cove doesn't have an actual sushi restaurant of its own to capitalize on their connection to the mouthwatering sashimi, but they *do* have the Bluefin Tuna Interpretation Centre, open during summer and featuring both a life-sized model of a bluefin and a gift shop offering many tuna-themed souvenirs.

BIG GARGANTUAN & RIDICULOUSLY OVERSIZED

The largest bluefin ever landed was 677 kilograms, dragged out of the water by a presumably exhausted Nova Scotian named Ken Fraser in 1979. The women's record is held by Collette Perras, who caught a bluefin that tipped the scales at 530 kilograms in the same waters the previous year.

Weird Weather of Atlantic Canada

Fair is foul, and foul is fair:
Hover through the fog and filthy air.

–The Weird Sisters, *Macbeth*

Mother Nature can be far from maternal sometimes,
particularly in Atlantic Canada. Deadly hurricanes, floods
and ice storms are all her little ways of letting us know that,
deep down inside, she really hates us. Or perhaps really bad
weather is just her way of getting revenge for all those times
people chopped down a forest to build a Walmart.

In any event, they say that if you don't like the weather in
Atlantic Canada, just wait a few minutes and it will
change. Actually, people say that about a lot of places, but
at least here it's with good reason.

WEATHERING THE WEATHER
St. John's, Newfoundland

Newfoundland's capital city is famous for a number of things—for being the oldest occupied settlement in North America, and for having the most bars per square kilometre than any other city in the world—but it is mainly known for having some of the weirdest weather in the country.

St. John's has the dubious distinction of being the foggiest, the windiest, the cloudiest, the snowiest *and* the rainiest major city in Canada. According to Environment Canada, the city is socked in with fog approximately 124 days a year (narrowly beating out hazy Halifax by two whole days); the winds, on

average, blow at around 24 kilometres per hour; and the sun only peeks through the clouds for a brief 1500 hours a year. Residents also have to shovel around 4 metres of snow off their driveways per year and splash through 1500 millimetres of rain.

In fact, the weather in Newfoundland is generally so awful that residents have invented their own language to describe it. Just like the Inuit are said to have a hundred different words for snow, so too do Newfoundlanders have plenty of words to describe the weather. Some of the more colourful examples include:

Airsome:	cold, bracing
Civil:	a lack of wind
Dally:	a sudden lull
Dwye:	a brief downpour or storm
Faffering:	blowing in sudden gusts
Fairy squall:	sudden strong winds on an otherwise civil day
In wind:	winds coming in from the sea
Liner:	strong winds during the equinox
Lun:	winds stopping
Norther:	freezing cold wind coming from the north
Out wind:	winds blowing out to sea
Scud:	a strong gust
Screecher:	a howling storm
Sheila's brush:	a seemingly inevitable fierce storm in late March
Shuff:	yet another word for a strong gust
Smoke:	gusts of wind and spray
Stun breeze:	sea winds of 20 to 25 knots
Weatherish:	cloudy skies portending rain

BUMMER OF '69

Some of your readers may probably be incredulous as to weather warnings, given so long an interval before an expected danger.

–Stephen Saxby, 1868

In 1868, back when the science of meteorology was in its infancy and predicting the upcoming week's weather was mostly guesswork, a man named Stephen Saxby, a lieutenant in the British navy and amateur astronomer, sent several dire letters to local newspapers in which he predicted that a devastating storm with massive tides would occur in the North Atlantic exactly one year later—on October 5, 1869. Saxby was vague as to the exact location of the storm and was widely dismissed as a nutcase, as most people who send doom-and-gloom letters to newspapers usually are.

However, late in the afternoon of October 4, 1869—only one day before Saxby's predicted deadline—a hurricane hit the Bay of Fundy region and caused a 2-metre-high storm surge that breached protective dikes and flooded inland areas. Countless ships were destroyed on wharfs and breakwaters, and more than a hundred people were killed. The storm—which came to be called the "Saxby Gale" despite having happened back in the days before hurricanes were named—also created the highest tidal level ever measured at Nova Scotia's Burntcoat Head—an impressive 21.6 metres above sea level.

Stranger still, the accuracy of Saxby's forecast owed more to luck (if you can call it that) than to science. Even though the alignment of the sun and moon explained the unusually high tides, which the Bay of Fundy tends to have anyway, it doesn't account for the occurrence of the storm itself.

THIS PLACE BLOWS
WRECKHOUSE, NEWFOUNDLAND

Newfoundland has a park, a village, a mountain range and over a dozen other places that are called either Blow Me Down or its variant, Blomidon, for the mighty winds that buffet the rocky coast. But one place in particular, the Channel-Port aux Basques region, has earned itself the nickname "Wreckhouse" for the hurricane-strength gusts that regularly hit the area.

Local legend has it that Wreckhouse is the second windiest place in the world after Antarctica—the winds have been known to gust in excess of 200 kilometres per hour, strong enough to easily tip over trains and tractor trailers and, yes, even wreck houses.

Channel-Port aux Basques, located on the southeast tip of Newfoundland, is one of two main entry points to the province by sea, and the Wreckhouse winds are its gatekeeper: as soon as you get off the ferry, you have to make it past them.

The distinctive geography causes the phenomenon: the Wreckhouse region is a large expanse of flat, treeless land running between the sea and the Long Range Mountains. Southeast winds are funnelled through the mountains and build up pressure as they are squeezed into narrow gulches in the rock. Once cut loose into the valley, the winds can gain enough speed to equal a Category-2 hurricane. Mind you, hundreds of tourists drive through Wreckhouse every year without ever encountering this blustery phenomenon because southeasterlies are, by far, the worst in winter, which isn't the time of year tourists tend to visit the Rock anyway.

Like most things in Newfoundland, Wreckhouse has a strange tale attached to it. In the days when trains still ran through the region, the Wreckhouse miles were considered the dangerous stretch. In 1939, the railway company—sick of having their trains blown off the tracks—hired a local trapper named Lockie MacDougall to advise them of the wind conditions. MacDougall is said to have had the freakish ability to sense wind conditions in advance and would send warnings to the train conductors when the going wasn't good. Up until his death in 1965, he delayed hundreds of trains and likely saved just as many lives during his tenure as a self-proclaimed "human wind gauge."

DID YOU  KNOW?

The least windy place in all of Canada can also be found in Atlantic Canada. Sleepy Summerside, Prince Edward Island, generally sees average breezes of around 4.4 kilometres per hour. Needless to say, you don't see many sailboats in its harbour or kites being flown on its famous beaches.

THE SPIES WHO WENT OUT INTO THE COLD
MARTIN'S BAY, LABRADOR

Canada is a big country. How big is it? I'm glad you asked. It's *so* big that it took nearly 40 years before anyone realized the Nazis had successfully invaded Canada during World War II.

In October 1943, the crew of the German submarine *U-537* made the one and only armed landing on North American soil at remote Martin's Bay in northern Labrador. The German's reason for choosing this seemingly unlikely military target was because the sub was loaded with a Siemens mobile weather station called the WFL-26, nicknamed "Kurt" after the mission's leader, Dr. Kurt Sommermeyer.

Weather systems in the Northern Hemisphere generally move from west to east, which gave the Allied forces a distinct advantage at sea because they could predict the weather far more accurately than the Germans.

Using the dense Labrador fog as cover from potential air patrols, the Germans set up the transmitter on a high point overlooking the Atlantic. They then hung a sign stating that Kurt belonged to the "Canadian Weather Service" and quickly *das booted* it out of there again.

But, unfortunately for the Nazis (now *there* is a sentence you don't come across too often), the automated station only broadcast weather reports for a few days before falling silent, most likely killed by the Labrador cold. A second submarine was sent to conduct repairs but was sunk en route by Allied torpedoes, which meant it was curtains for Kurt.

And so the supposed spy station sat silent until the '70s, when a retired German engineer—having gone through Sommermeyer's papers while researching a history book—wrote to the Canadian government inquiring about the weather station's fate. No one had the slightest idea what he was talking about. He then forwarded a copy of *U-537*'s logbook, which contained the transmitter's exact location, and a military expedition was subsequently sent out to recover Kurt in 1981. The largely intact station was brought back to Ottawa and now has a new home in the Canadian War Museum, where it continues to *not* broadcast weather reports back to Germany.

DID YOU KNOW?

Although several sunken Nazi subs have been discovered in U.S. waters ranging from New Jersey south to Florida, the only U-boat ever downed in Canadian waters was discovered in 2004 about 200 kilometres off Nova Scotia's coast. The *U-215* was sunk after torpedoing and sinking the American ship *USS Alexander Macomb*, which was en route to Russia to bring war supplies to the troops. The German sub was supposed to be carrying out a secret mission to lay mines in Boston Harbor at the time, but it seems the sub's commander, Fritz Höckner, couldn't resist sinking the *Macomb*, which alerted a nearby British warship, the *HMS Le Tigre*, to its presence and sent the U-Boat to the bottom.

JUAN FOR THE RECORD BOOKS

The worst storm to hit Atlantic Canada in over a century happened on September 29, 2003. Hurricane Juan was a Category-2 hurricane with wind speeds topping 165 kilometres per hour, which caused eight deaths and over $200 million in damages in Nova Scotia alone. Wave-riding weather buoys off the entrance of Halifax Harbour were snapped from their moorings after recording waves in excess of 20 metres high. Nearly three-quarters of the trees in Halifax's prized Point Pleasant Park were blown down, and one-third of the homes in the area filed some sort of insurance claim.

Odd Outdoor Sports
in Atlantic Canada

As with most places in Canada, hockey is huge here too, and there are at least two places in Atlantic Canada with particularly interesting connections to the game. But while the hockey-mad Canadian cliché rings true, there are still plenty of other outdoor pastimes people pursue, some decidedly on the stranger side of things.

QUIDI PRIDE
QUIDI VIDI LAKE, NEWFOUNDLAND

The city of St. John's is home to an event that is both the oldest ongoing sporting event in North American history as well as the biggest annual party on the island.

The Royal St. John's Regatta was first held, officially, on August 12, 1816, in the city's famous sheltered harbour to celebrate the anniversary of the coronation of King George VIII, but it is very likely that European fishermen and sailors had been holding unofficial regattas here for at least a century before that. A decade later, the race moved to Quidi Vidi Lake (pronounced "kitty vitty" and likely derived from the Latin phrase *Que divide*, which means "here divides") in the city's east end, where it has been held on the first Wednesday of August ever since.

Regatta Day is the only public holiday in Canada that depends on the weather: the decision to postpone the regatta is made by unelected officials on the day of the event. If it is raining or too windy, the holiday is simply put off until the following day.

In the olden days, the boat races were held over three days with ancient gigs, yawls and long boats manned by beefy boatmen, and there was serious money at stake. Nowadays, the event attracts more female competitors than male.

The regatta, which attracts about 40,000 spectators each year, is one of the more unusual of its kind. Teams of six compete in 16-metre fixed-seat racing shells built to the same specifications that were used centuries ago and, instead of simply racing in a straight line like other boat races, the 2.6 kilometre course has competitors rounding slalom gates and buoys.

SQUASH RACKET
WINDSOR, NOVA SCOTIA

While the Royal St. John's Regatta may be the oldest, it is far from the strangest of Atlantic Canada's annual boat races. That honour belongs hands-down to Windsor's Pumpkin Regatta, in which paddlers riding giant hollowed-out pumpkins race each other across Lake Pezaquid.

Pumpkins have always been big in this corner of Nova Scotia, and gourd growers from across Atlantic Canada and New England have been gathering every October at Lake Pezaquid for decades to see whose is biggest. Local farmer Howard Dill is a four-time *Guinness Book of World Records* holder for his massive pumpkins and, with his patented Dill's Atlantic Giant pumpkin seeds, is credited with launching the international craze of growing super-sized squashes.

In 1999, Windsor decided to declare itself "the Pumpkin Capital of the World" and launched the inaugural Great Pumpkin Race to draw attention to the bold initiative. Around 2000 skeptical souls showed up to watch five pumpkin pilots paddle their way into history. The winner covered the one-kilometre distance in just over 13 minutes.

Since then, the annual event has grown and grown. It drew greater international attention in 2005 when American home-maker extraordinaire Martha Stewart announced her intention

to enter the race. Unfortunately, as a convicted felon, she was ineligible to come to Canada even for such a notable cause.

Several cabinet ministers then took up Martha's case, including then-public works minister Scott Brison, Member of Parliament for the Windsor area and also a former regatta winner. Stockwell Day, who was the Conservative Party's foreign affairs spokesman, demanded to know what the problem was, asking: "Are they afraid she'll throw her apple pies at us, or maybe wrap us up in her prison poncho?"

In the end, an exception was made and a visa was granted for Martha, but as it turned out, on the day she was scheduled to arrive, her private plane ended up getting stuck in Maine because of heavy fog, and Windsor pumpkin enthusiasts had to make do with one of her underlings taking part instead.

EARLY HURLY
LONG POND, NOVA SCOTIA

... boys let out racin', yelpin', hollerin', and whoopin' like mad with pleasure, and the play-ground, and the games at base in the fields, or hurly on the long pond on the ice ...

–Thomas Chandler Haliburton, "The Attaché"

Of course, being a primo pumpkin-racing destination is far from Windsor's only claim to sporting fame. About the only thing hockey fans enjoy more than a good hockey fight is fighting over where the good old hockey game began. Numerous books have been published over the years making the case for different cities, and old novels, letters, paintings and even wooden pucks have been held up as evidence. Claims have been made for the cities of Dartmouth, Montréal and Kingston, as well as for the tiny Northwest Territory backwater of Déline, but the most compelling argument is that Long Pond, located just outside of Windsor, Nova Scotia, is where the first Canadian puck was dropped. Windsor's claim is based on an 1836 story, "The Attaché," by local author Thomas Chandler

Haliburton (1796–1865) in which the main character Sam Slick describes boys playing "hurly on the long pond on the ice," apparently a recollection of the author's own early days of playing a hockey-like game while a student at King's College in Halifax.

ON FROZEN POND
PLASTER ROCK, NEW BRUNSWICK

While the town of Windsor may hold bragging rights for being the Canadian home of pond hockey, Plaster Rock is carrying on the tradition. This community in northwestern New Brunswick recently put itself on the world map by hosting the annual World Pond Hockey Championships. The event takes place every February, during the NHL All-Star break, with players gathering in this tiny town on the Tobique River to play hockey the way it was meant to be played—on uneven natural ice in the freezing cold and with a few beers, if so inclined. After a modest debut in 2002 that saw 40 mostly Canadian teams compete, the event has grown to include more than 120 teams from around the world.

The three-day tournament features four-man teams (so far, it remains a boys-only affair) competing in as many as 20 simultaneous games on makeshift rinks about a third the size of NHL ice, with each game lasting around 30 minutes.

At stake are lifelong bragging rights, possible puck-bunnies and a wooden replica of Lord Stanley's Mug made out of maple. Prime Minister and noted hockey-enthusiast Stephen Harper even came to town in 2007 to drop the puck at the ceremonial opening face-off, the first time a prime minister has ever visited Plaster Rock.

In its purest form, pond hockey in Atlantic Canada has almost no rules, though bodychecking and lifting the puck are generally frowned upon. You simply drop a pair of boots or a pile of

clothes at each end of the ice to make the goalposts, and there are no out-of-bounds except where the ice runs out or the snow piles up. You play with as many, or as few, people as happen to show up. There are no timeouts, penalties or power plays—you play until it's dark, until your mother/wife/partner calls you in for supper or until you can't feel your toes anymore. And usually nobody remembers to keep track of the score.

**GARGANTUAN &
RIDICULOUSLY
OVERSIZED**

Plaster Rock is home to the world's largest fiddlehead, a 7.3-metre tall wooden sculpture erected to honour a local delicacy which—if you're not from New Brunswick and have never heard of fiddleheads—are the edible fronds of wild ferns. Speaking from experience, I'd say they are an acquired taste.

GOLFING A GULF

AROOSTOOK VALLEY COUNTRY CLUB, NEW BRUNSWICK/MAINE

There is probably only one course on earth where golfers are not only able to drive balls into a different country, but into a different time zone entirely. However, this one-of-a-kind course's days may be numbered thanks to lingering post-9/11 hysteria.

The Aroostook Valley Country Club, whose membership is divided between citizens from both Canada and the United States, is on the New Brunswick side of the border near Perth-Andover, but its entrance and parking lot are located in Maine. For nearly a century, golfers have used a small country road on the American side of the border to reach the club's entrance.

But with no checkpoint on the road, Big Brother has no way of knowing who or what is crossing back and forth between the two countries. It could be anything: cheap prescription drugs, weapons of mass destruction, al-Qaeda operatives or even Martha Stewart.

In early 2008, the club received their first letter of warning from the feds. As the owners summed it up on their website:

> *It is now official that the U.S. Department of Homeland (in)Security has determined that the Brown Road/Russell Road is a gaping hole in their border and is a terrorist threat. No mention of the other thousands of miles of unprotected border between Canada and the U.S.*

As this book was going to press, bored border officials were set to be stationed on the remote road, and anyone trying to get in a few rounds of golf would be ordered to take the 33 kilometre detour to the Fort Fairfield crossing, where hopefully their clubs wouldn't be considered potentially deadly weapons and confiscated.

HANG MINUS TEN
LAWRENCETOWN BEACH, NOVA SCOTIA

Most people don't think of Canada when they think about surfing. If they do, they're probably thinking about Tofino, Sombrio Beach, River Jordan or some other Pacific break off the west coast of Vancouver Island, not anywhere on the Atlantic side.

In fact, Nova Scotia has some truly kick-ass surfing spots, the most famous of which is Lawrencetown Beach, a south-facing stretch of sand that runs for nearly 1.5 kilometres and is located only 30 minutes from downtown Halifax. The province has two natural advantages when it come to catching waves: a coastline exposed to the open ocean with no barrier islands or reefs to slow down incoming swells, and plenty of long peninsulas and bays. The peninsulas create "point breaks" that focus the energy of the swell and protect surfers from the wind, while the rocky coastline makes sure that the surf will be sweet somewhere, regardless of the wave and wind direction. Waves off the coast of Nova Scotia can be as large as 4 metres tall.

The only catch (and it's a big one) is that the surfing is the best during the dead of winter—snowstorms and howling winds are often the forecasts that have local surfers heading for the beach. Water temperatures from October to April vary from 0° to 7°C, compared to the summer months when a good day can see the water as warm as 20°C.

Surfing in such extreme temperatures is made possible only by heavy-duty wetsuits that feature built-in hoods and shielded zippers, super-flexible joints, a fleece lining and at least 6 milli-metres of neoprene. With the addition of thick boots and gloves, the only skin left exposed to the elements is the face—which can still be more than enough to trigger a killer ice cream headache after a wipeout.

But aside from the cold water, heavy fogs, dangerous riptides, the lack of lifeguards and random floating chunks of ice, the real danger of winter surfing isn't *in* the water, but *out* of it. There are no heated changing rooms or bathrooms to retreat to when it comes time to rip off the wetsuit and change. Surfers' extremities have only a few minutes of functionality after they strip off the wetsuit and, if they don't move fast enough, their hands will freeze, making it near impossible to unlock the car and crank the heat.

It may sound crazy, but then again it is not like there are many snowboarding options in the area.

BOTTOM OF THE HILLS
BROOKVALE WINTER ACTIVITY PARK, PRINCE EDWARD ISLAND

As I mentioned above, Atlantic Canada isn't particularly famous for its downhill skiing and snowboarding scene. Apart from the Marble Mountain resort in western Newfoundland, mountains are generally molehills in this part of the country

and nowhere more so than on PEI, a province flatter than the beer at the bottom of a week-old keg and whose modest 140-metre summit is the site of a potato patch. So it is more than just a little weird that anyone bothered to build a down-hill ski resort at all.

Brookvale boasts a vertical drop of 76 metres from top to bottom—that's 250 feet for any of you American readers planning a future winter ski vacation. For some perspective, this is roughly 10 metres lower than the Kingdom of Dubai's infamous indoor ski resort, or just slightly higher than the highest point of the Confederation Bridge.

To be fair, Brookvale does receive around 250 centimetres of snow each year and offers a half-pipe and terrain park, but somehow it is hard to believe that 30 percent of the trails, as claimed on the park's website, can only be ridden by "advanced and expert" skiers and boarders.

THE SLIGHT CLIFFS OF DOVER
DOVER ISLAND, NOVA SCOTIA

On any given summer's day, this small, rocky island in Halifax Harbour can find itself literally covered with people wearing uncomfortably tight footwear and sporting chalk-covered hands, dangling from their bleeding fingertips on one of its many cliffs and boulders.

Dover Island, which has no direct ferry service, is considered to be one of the best bouldering spots in Atlantic Canada. The sport is the much-maligned cousin of traditional mountain climbing and rock climbing—only without the same level of danger. More gymnastic than it is gravity-defying, bouldering is basically untethered climbing that sticks close to the ground, often with climbers moving sideways instead of up and down.

Bouldering began as a means for climbers to train and has since evolved into a legitimate sport in its own right. You don't need tons of expensive technical gear or even a partner—just a desire to challenge yourself and nature by solving "problems," referring to a series of "moves" to get from one point on the rock to another.

Dover Island is home to over 100 bouldering problems—featuring such colourful names as Orangutan, Orgasmatron and I Heel Good—ranging from something your grandmother could crank to moves that would give your friendly neighbourhood Spiderman pause. The island is also home to an annual Boulderfest competition each summer, which generally sells out in a matter of hours.

A LEAGUE OF THEIR OWN
CHARLOTTETOWN, PRINCE EDWARD ISLAND

Do you think softball is only for weekend wannabe warriors or other athletic softies? Try telling that to the hardy softball players who turned out at Charlottetown's Central Field baseball diamond in late June 2008 to set a world record for the longest softball game in history.

It took 96 hours and 467 beer-free innings for the team from Mark's Work Wearhouse to beat Hunter's Ale House 1066–874, while simultaneously beating a previous Guinness World Record set in Dollard-des-Ormeaux, Québec, by a good half hour.

There were a total of 40 participants and 20 players on the ice at all times, with lines of 10 players per team taking shifts. Mother Nature didn't cooperate either, plaguing them with heavy rains, not-so-distant thunder and temperatures that never rose above 14 °C.

At the time *Weird Places in Atlantic Canada* went to print, the record had yet to be officially recognized by the *Guinness Book of World Records*, though it has been given the thumbs up from the lesser known worldrecordsacademy.org. The Guinness honchos initially wanted $21,000 to fly over and house their officials while they verified the event, but such a large outlay of cash would have gone against the event's additional goal of raising money for the Canadian Cancer Society, which ended up totalling $10,000.

Strange Settlement Names of Atlantic Canada

Eastern Canada has some of the most colourful settlement names in the country. Long before the Vikings ever set foot in Vinland, the First Nation tribes, accomplished explorers in their own right, had been naming places all through Atlantic Canada.

Early European arrivals must have figured it was easier to accept the often unpronounceable names rather than create their own. Many of these names have survived not only the centuries and a slew of translations, but also several attempts at cultural assimilation. Sometimes the meaning can be lost in translation when English, French, Basque, Spanish, Portuguese and Mi'kmaq words are tossed into a blender and then left to commingle.

As a result of this linguistic potpourri, Atlantic Canada boasts a large number of places that appear on worldwide lists of weird place names. They range from the overly multi-syllabic, the sexually suggestive or the unintentionally ironic to the pathetically prosaic, the majorly mysterious and, as you would expect, the downright weird. Here are a few of my personal favourites.

Annapolis Royal, Nova Scotia

A typical East Coast mélange of French and English (and even Greek), this small town in southwestern Nova Scotia is located on the site where French explorer Samuel de Champlain established Port Royal, North America's first permanent European settlement, way back in 1604.

After the Brits got their hands on Port Royal a century later, it was renamed Annapolis in honour of their beloved Queen Anne and the Greek word for city (*polis*). The decision to tack Royal back onto the name was grudgingly made in 1903, seeing as no matter how hard they tried Royal was the only name people would ever use to refer to the port town.

A gravestone in the local cemetery marking the final resting place of one Bethiah Douglas, who kicked the bucket in 1710, is the oldest in Canada. It is also home the Annapolis Royal Generating Station, a power plant that uses the Bay of Fundy's famous tides to generate electricity.

Antigonish, Nova Scotia

The first recorded use of this name was "Articougnesche," likely derived from the Mi'kmaq word *nalegitkoonech*, which means either (depending on which Mi'kmaq you happen to ask) "flowing through a marsh" or "where branches are torn off by bears gathering beechnuts."

Antigonish is home to Saint Francis Xavier University—better known as St. FX (and properly slurred as "Sayneffecks")—whose distinguished alumnae include the likes of Mike Smith (Bubbles of *Trailer Park Boys* fame), the late hockey colour commentator Danny Gallivan and former Prime Minister Brian Mulroney.

Antigonish also hosts the annual Highlands Games, the oldest event of its kind in Canada and a celebration of Scottish culture that revolves around men in skirts lifting and/or hurling heavy objects through the air.

Many Nova Scotians, particularly residents of Antigonish themselves (Antigonishians? Antigonishites? Antigonishers?), are generally pro-Antigonish.

BAGDAD, NEW BRUNSWICK

The handful of residents in this small community east of Sussex were no doubt relieved when they didn't find themselves accidentally shocked and/or awed when George W. Bush launched his ill-advised search for missing weapons of mass destruction in 2003.

BARENEED, NEWFOUNDLAND

The rather desperate sounding name for this village near Bay Roberts was originally closer to Barren Head or Bearing Head, but due to the strong accents of early settlers, it came to be pronounced something like "Bareneed." The village currently has a bare need for residents to stop leaving town.

BEERSVILLE, NEW BRUNSWICK

Unfortunately, according to Beersville's online community profile, there isn't actually anywhere in this small village north of

Moncton to buy beer. Although this may seem like one of the worst cases of blatant false advertising since *The Neverending Story*, Beersville was instead named for the descendants of early settlers Robert and Phoebe Beers rather than for having a strong thirst for suds.

BLACKHEAD, NEWFOUNDLAND

Not much more than a pimple on the shores of Conception Bay, Blackhead found itself squeezed into an amalgamated town called "Small Point-Adam's Cove-Blackhead-Broad Cove" in 1968. Blackhead's main claim to fame is being the spot of the very first Methodist church in Canada, which popped up in 1769.

BROOKLYN, NOVA SCOTIA

*But if God came here on Earth with us and asked if he could rest
I'd take him to my Nova Scotia home, the place that I love best.*

–Hank Snow, "My Nova Scotia Home"

This lesser-known Brooklyn in Queen's County was put on the
map in 1907 when the railway opened between Yarmouth and
Halifax. It is best known as the birthplace of country musician
Hank Snow, who fled an abusive home at age 12 and never
actually returned. They even have a Brooklyn bridge of their
own spanning the Mersey River, but it isn't for sale or nearly
as impressive as the one that leads into Manhattan.

BUMBLEBEE BIGHT, NEWFOUNDLAND

Bees actually sting rather than bite, but in any case, this had
nothing to do with how this town on Pilley's Island in Notre
Dame Bay got its name. Founded in the 1860s, the town was
once home to one of Newfoundland's largest deposits of pyrite,
a material also known as "fool's gold" that is yellow and often
streaked with black, not unlike a bumblebee itself.

The mine became the first of its kind in Newfoundland to be
equipped with electricity, and the town soon became a major
commercial hub with its very own hotel, courthouse and the
area's only hospital. However, the mine shut down in 1908
after it ran out of ore, so the residents turned to fishing. Then
they ran out of fish, which probably stung.

BURNT CHURCH, NEW BRUNSWICK

During the Seven Years War, British troops destroyed pretty
much any Acadian and Mi'kmaq settlements they could find

in the Miramichi area. On September 17, 1758, Colonel James Murray wrote in his logbook that after "having two days hunted all around us for the Indians and Acadians to no purpose, we destroyed their provision, wigwams and houses. The church, a very handsome one built with stone, did not escape."

The village that was rebuilt on the site took its name from the remaining husk of said stone house of worship instead of keeping its original name *Eskinwobudich*, a Mi'kmaq word meaning "lookout place."

Nowadays, the town makes periodic headlines for occasional violent clashes between Mi'kmaq and non-Aboriginal fishermen over the ever-dwindling lobster stocks, though as of yet no more churches have been torched.

CAPE ST. GEORGE-PETIT JARDIN-GRAND JARDIN-DE GRAU-MARCHES POINT-LORETTO, NEWFOUNDLAND

Cape St. George-Petit Jardin-Grand Jardin-De Grau-Marches Point-Loretto, located on the Port au Port Peninsula, once had the claim to fame of having the second-longest place name in all of Canada. Sadly, exasperated residents decided in 1969 to shorten their hippopotomonstrosesquipedalian name to something with less floccinaucinihilipilification, deciding on simply "Cape St. George."

The overall Canadian champion with the longest name—the Ontario township municipality of "Dysart, Dudley, Harcourt, Guilford, Harburn, Bruton, Havelock, Eyre and Clyde"—only beat Cape St. George-Petit Jardin-Grand Jardin-De Grau-Marches Point-Loretto by a mere three letters.

Feel free to count them yourself if you don't believe me.

CANSO, NOVA SCOTIA

This can-do village on the eastern edge of mainland Nova Scotia was once home to one of the largest fish processing plants in the world before the bottom fell out of the industry. It is best known today for having the world's deepest causeway named after it (see Bizarre Bridges), for hosting "Stanfest" (an annual music festival in honour of the late semi-local folk-singing icon Stan Rogers) and for having a crater on the planet Mars named after it. Canso takes its name from the Mi'kmaq word *kamsok*, meaning "by the big cliff," a reference to the bluffs of Chebucto Bay.

CARDIGAN, PRINCE EDWARD ISLAND

Cardigans are best known today for being a type of button-down sweater popular not only among senior citizens but also with trendy hipsters, who combine it with t-shirts for a more chic, layered look. Cardigans, like the PEI village, were named for a British military commander named James Brudenell, the Earl of Cardigan, better known as the guy behind the disastrous Charge of the Light Brigade during the Crimea War's Battle of Balaclava—an event that, coincidentally, inspired yet another cozy garment, the face-hugging balaclava.

Originally named Cardigan Bridge, this small Kings County fishing community currently holds the accolades for having the smallest public library in all of Canada.

CENTRAL LOT 16, PRINCE EDWARD ISLAND

The seemingly unimaginative "Central Lot 16" is a leftover from the 18th century, when surveyor Samuel Holland divvied up the island into a grid made up of lots and lots of lots. For whatever reason, the residents of Central Lot 16 simply never got around to coming up with a better name for their town, unlike every single other community on the island.

COCAGNE, NEW BRUNSWICK

This coastal community on the Northumberland Strait takes its name from the mythical "Cockaigne," a glutton's paradise from medieval French literature where rivers run with wine, houses are made of sugar cakes and streets are paved with pastry, an image that was the inspiration behind the famous folk song "Big Rock Candy Mountain."

Any Mandrake the Magician fans out there might also remember Cockaigne as being the kingdom of Princess Narda.

Despite being named for a utopian paradise, Cocagne has found itself struggling in recent years to provide its residents with clean drinking water. As there is no municipal sewer system in the village, the overloaded septic systems, which are often located beside wells, have been blamed for a rash of outbreaks of fecal coliforms.

Cocagne is also home to Canadian Olympic bobsledder Serge Despres, who was suspended in August 2008 for 20 months because of illicit drug use. As much as I'd love to crack a joke here about how a snow enthusiast from Cocagne managed to blow his chances and put his career behind the eight ball because of cocaine use, the illicit drugs in question were actually steroids.

COME BY CHANCE, NEWFOUNDLAND

But my languid mood forsook me, when
I found a name that took me,
Quite by chance I came across it,
'Come-by-Chance' was what I read

–Banjo Paterson, "Come By Chance"

It's not that the residents of Come By Chance only sporadically manage to climax.

Instead, this town on the north end of the Isthmus of Avalon most likely got its odd name because it used to be a chancy proposition for fishermen to try and bring their boats ashore here in bad weather, which—being a fairly busy port—was actually more often than not in Come By Chance.

The town is also home to Newfoundland's one and only oil refinery, the North Atlantic Refining Company, which pumps out around 115,000 barrels a day.

As chance would have it, there is yet another place with this same unusual name, located in Australia. A sheep station in northern New South Wales was named Come By Chance after the owners surprised themselves and others by buying the place.

COW HEAD, NEWFOUNDLAND

While it sounds like a hurled schoolyard insult or perhaps an alternative name for mad cow disease, this small town on the coast of the Great Northern Peninsula was actually named for a cow-shaped boulder that has since rolled into the sea.

The village briefly made national headlines in 2008 when Prime Minister Harper's wife Laureen happened to be in town and was so taken with a play she attended, called *Tempting*

Paradise, that she went backstage to meet the cast after the show. One of the actors, Deidre Gillard-Rowlings, felt obliged to point out to her that the play she had so thoroughly enjoyed, which had also toured successfully overseas, had only been made possible because of an arts grant program that her husband had recently cut out of the budget.

CRAPAUD, PRINCE EDWARD ISLAND

Pronounced "Crappo," this PEI village has been the butt of jokes for years. Crapaud takes its name from the early French name for the nearby Westmoreland River, *Rivière aux Crapauds*, meaning "river of toads," which was a somewhat misleading name given that the stream isn't teaming with toads so much as eels, which in French are known as *crapauds de mer* or sea toads.

CUPIDS, NEWFOUNDLAND

The fact that there is a village named Cupids on the shores of Conception Bay happens to be a coincidence. The first permanent British colony in Canada, established by a guy named John Guy in 1610, was originally called Coopers after the guys

who cut down trees to make staves, which are used to construct barrels for pickling fish. Either way, it seems as though Cupid himself must have put in an early appearance because it was here, on March 27, 1613, that the first English child was born on what would become Canadian soil.

DILDO, NEWFOUNDLAND

Don't let the names deceive you, Newfoundland's mighty fine,
So spend a night on Dildo if you think you've got the time.

–The Arrogant Worms, "One Night On Dildo"

This fishing village on the east side of Trinity Bay gets perennial mentions on lists of other snicker-inducing places, like Nova Scotia's Shag Harbour, the state of Pennsylvania's Intercourse and the unfortunately named Austrian city of F***ing.

Consistently voted as one of Canada's prettiest villages, Dildo was founded in 1700 and probably got its suggestive name because "dildo" was the old English word for the tubular pins that held oars in place while rowing. Or maybe the local vegetation reminded a homesick early settler of the Dildo cactus (*Cephalocereus millspaughii*). Or maybe it is simply yet another misspelled or mistranslated version of a word that had a wholly different meaning in another language.

Dildo was also once simply a synonym for "cylinder," which is what Dildo Harbour resembles (among other things). Get your mind out of the gutter. Admittedly, this would be easier to do if the village wasn't located just across the bay from Spread Eagle. Or so close to South Dildo. Or, for that matter, if the high school mascot wasn't named Woody.

DINGWALL, NOVA SCOTIA

A friend of mine used to date a girl named Debbie from this northern village in Cape Breton. Only he never called her simply by her name; she was always "Debbie from Dingwall" because it was more fun to say. Maybe this is part of why they broke up.

In any case, the town once had the more sensible-sounding name "Young's Cove" before being renamed after its first postmaster, Robert Dingwall.

Located just north of the Cape Breton Highlands National Park, Dingwall has only 600 or so permanent residents, but their ranks swell immensely during the summer months when the town sees an influx of tourists and wealthy mainlanders who have summer homes in the area.

ECUM SECUM, NOVA SCOTIA

Pronounced "EEE-kum SEE-kum," this rural community on the Eastern Shore is named after yet another lost Mi'kmaq word, originally spelled *Ekamsagen* and possibly meaning "red house," and is simply fun to say out loud. Just try it.

EUREKA, NOVA SCOTIA

Eureka!

–Archimedes

The famous Greek mathematician is said to have shouted this famous exclamation—meaning "I have found it!"—after easing into a bathtub and noticing that the water level had risen, thereby discovering the principle of buoyancy. Since then, it has become synonymous with any sudden flash of genius.

Currently, *Eureka* is also the name of a television series starring an old college buddy of mine (shout out to Molson Hall's Colin Ferguson!) about a small town in Oregon where everyone is a genius secretly working for the U.S. government. But this particular Eureka, a small town in Pictou County, is simply named for the Eureka Milling Company.

If any of the three hundred or so residents who reside there today are in fact geniuses, they're playing it close to their chests.

FERRYLAND, NEWFOUNDLAND

There aren't any ferries servicing Ferryland and, with a population in the low hundreds, probably not too many fairies either. While there is some disagreement over the origin of the name, Ferryland—called *Farilham* by Portuguese fishermen and *Forillon* by the French—was more than likely just anglicized to its current incarnation.

Ferryland is furthermore famous for featuring the alphanumerically lowest postal code in Canada, with addresses beginning at A0A.

FLORENCEVILLE, NEW BRUNSWICK

This town on the Saint John River was originally called Buttermilk Creek but was renamed in 1853 after British nurse extraordinaire Florence Nightingale, heroine of the Crimean War and founder of modern nursing. It is now the headquarters for McCain Foods Limited, the world's largest producer of frozen french fries, themselves a contributing factor to the worldwide need for nurses.

GAMBO, NEWFOUNDLAND

Nobody really knows why Gambo is called Gambo. Located around 300 kilometres from St. John's, it is best known as being the former home of "the little guy from Gambo," Premier Joey Smallwood, a polarizing provincial politician and the final father of Confederation who dragged Newfoundland kicking and screaming into Canada in 1949. Gambo has since erected a statue, which is neither small nor wooden, in its most famous son's honour.

GARDEN OF EDEN, NOVA SCOTIA

The biblical Garden of Eden is thought to have been located at the headwaters of the Euphrates River, but if your idea of paradise isn't to be found in modern day Iraq, then there is always a backup Garden of Eden around 30 kilometres southwest of Antigonish.

This village in Pictou County was first settled in 1830 by a man named William MacDonald, who was so struck by the region's natural beauty that he began to refer to himself as "Adam in the Garden." Presumably he had an "Eve" to keep him company, as there are more than a few McDonalds currently listed in the local phone book.

GARGAMELLE, NEWFOUNDLAND

More than just the nefarious nemesis of the Smurfs, Gargamelle is also a small community northwest of Port Saunders—not to mention being the name for the mother of the giant Gargantua from the 16th-century satire *Gargantua and Pantagrulle*, from which the word "gargantuan" (oft-used in this book) is derived.

GLENELG, NOVA SCOTIA

This village in Guyborough County has the distinction of having one of the most commonplace palindromes (where something can be read the same forward as it can be backward) in the world. The town is named after Lord Glenelg, who was the British Colonial Secretary in the 1830s, and consequently there are quite a few Glenelgs scattered around English-speaking corners of the globe, including in a township in Ontario, a village in Scotland, a town in Maryland and a suburb of Adelaide in South Australia.

They say that the *level* of *civic* pride for both *sexes* in *Glenelg*, perhaps because of living in a palindrome, is *never odd or even*. *Dammit I'm mad* that I can't think of any more palindrome jokes to use here.

GORE, NOVA SCOTIA

This farming community in Hants County got its name from the surname of a former lieutenant governor and not from any particular gory incident, which is the truth if not a particularly inconvenient one. Its main claim to fame is being the location of an Environment Canada weather radar station and for hosting a famous annual mountain bike race known as "Gore Fest."

GREAT VILLAGE, NOVA SCOTIA

What's so great about Great Village? Not a lot, really. This town of 500 or so souls on the shore of Cobequid Bay near Truro, however, does have a link to Pulitzer Prize-winning author Elizabeth Bishop (1911–1979), who lived there with her grandparents as a young girl after her father died and her mom was permanently institutionalized. She went on to base many of her stories around life in a fictional village of the same name, including her famous short story "In The Village."

GREENWICH, NEW BRUNSWICK
GREENWICH, NOVA SCOTIA
GREENWICH, PRINCE EDWARD ISLAND

It is pronounced "GREEN-wich" in New Brunswick, "GREE-nich" in Nova Scotia and "GREN-ich" in PEI. While the accent differs, all three share the exact same time zone—four hours behind Greenwich Mean Time (GMT-4)—so it's probably just as well there's no fifth Greenwich in Newfoundland with its own time zone to add to the confusion.

Grosses Coques, Nova Scotia

Bilingual types have been giggling over the double entendre for years, but this seaside community on the Bay of Fundy got its name for the large clams available at low tide rather than, you know, the *other* thing. However, an actual large cock can be found at 550 Main Street in the New Brunswick seaside town of Shediac, where the statue of a rooster stands proudly erect outside a Targett's Fried Chicken outlet.

Happy Adventure, Newfoundland

There are a number of possible explanations for the euphonious name of this outport village on the Eastport Peninsula. Some speculate it is a reflection of the joy that early settlers felt when they first arrived. (If so, it was presumably given before they spent their first winter there.) It might also commemorate the name of a ship that belonged to the dread pirate Peter Easton, or could perhaps be an expression of relief from someone who had just successfully hid from pirates in the maze of coves and channels lining the coast.

The likeliest explanation is that George Holbrook, a British hydrographer who surveyed Newman Sound in 1817, was happy to find shelter from a storm there.

The *Happy Adventure* was also the name of Farley Mowat's schooner in his 1968 book *The Boat Who Wouldn't Float*, an account of his misadventures sailing off the coast of Newfoundland. The famously uncooperative vessel currently sits dry-docked on a bluff overlooking Margaree Harbour in Cape Breton after the iconic author, who used to have a summer home in the area, finally washed his hands of the *Happy Adventure* and donated her to the city in 1990.

HAPPY VALLEY-GOOSE BAY, LABRADOR

Happy Valley-Goose Bay may be a bit of a mouthful, but you've got to admit that it sounds way more inviting than its former name: Refugee Cove. Now known as "The Hub of Labrador," the town got its start in 1941 when the military was looking for an alternate aerial shortcut to England rather than having to refuel at Gander Lake.

Built on a large sandy plateau at the western end of Lake Melville, Goose Bay airport was up and running in a few short months and briefly was the largest airport in North America. The name "Happy Valley" was given to the housing community built for the airport workers, possibly dubbed sarcastically seeing as how Labrador only has two seasons: winter and black-fly season. The two communities were finally amalgamated in 1975. Happy Valley-Goose Bay is home to CFB Goose Bay, still the largest military air base in northeastern North America.

HEAD OF ST. MARGARETS, NOVA SCOTIA

Unlike, say, Saint John the Baptist, who really did lose his head, Head of St. Margarets is named for being located at the head of St. Margarets Bay. For that matter, this particular "Saint" Margaret wasn't even a saint at all—the bay was named by explorer Samuel de Champlain for his mother, Marguerite.

HEART'S CONTENT, NEWFOUNDLAND

Like so many expressions today, the term "heart's content" first appeared in a play by William Shakespeare, who used it in both *Henry IV* and *The Merchant of Venice*.

Despite a heart's *actual* contents being mostly blood and ventricles, it has since come to refer to a feeling of happiness or contentment. This town on the Bay de Verde Peninsula off Trinity Bay is best known as being one of the terminus points for the first Transatlantic telegraph cable, completed in 1866, an event that caused nearby communities to rename themselves Heart's Desire and Heart's Delight.

HERRING NECK, NEWFOUNDLAND

Herrings themselves don't actually have a neck, and this fishing community on New World Island got its fishy name from the practice of early settlers who portaged loads of herring across the narrow neck of Pike's Arm to avoid its dangerous headwaters. It should also be noted that pikes don't have arms either.

JOE BATT'S ARM, NEWFOUNDLAND

Unlike pikes, Joe Batt did have arms—likely two of them, though the history books don't go into that much detail. This fishing village on the north shore of Fogo Island was named either for a thief who, in 1754, was sentenced to 15 lashes of a whip after stealing a pair of shoes, or for a sailor who helped Captain James Cook survey the area; or, quite possibly, they could both be one and the same person. An attempt was made in 1901 to rename the town Queenstown, but the new name never caught on and Joe Batt's Arm was quickly brought back into the fold.

KILBRIDE, NEWFOUNDLAND

Not what you would call a popular honeymoon destination, Kilbride is a suburb located on the south side of the city of St. John's. Named after the even more sinister-sounding Kilbride Falls on the nearby Waterford River, it is taken from the Irish phrase *Cill-Bhrigde*, which simply means "Brigid's Church."

KILLOWEEN, NEW BRUNSWICK

It may sound like a bad '80s horror movie, possibly one featuring an indestructible serial killer sporting a jack-o'-lantern mask, but this spooky-sounding town is simply a misspelled tribute to Charles Russell, Baron of Killowen, who was the Lord Chief Justice of England when the village was settled in 1894. Despite this decidedly non-spooky explanation, the town *is* said to have had a haunted covered bridge that was destroyed by fire in 2001.

The story goes that it was haunted by a woman whose decapitated body was discovered in the river below in 1890, but whose skull wasn't found until 37 years later when workers were digging new abutments in the riverbed. There had been many reports from travellers over the years of a headless woman dressed in black who would sit next to them in their carriage as they crossed the bridge.

KINKORA, PRINCE EDWARD ISLAND

Formerly called Somerset, this municipality northeast of Borden-Carleton—largely populated by Irish settlers—changed its name to Kinkora at the end of the 19th century to commemorate the ruins of the palace of the Irish king Brian Boru, who united Ireland in 1014. As you can plainly see, there is nothing remotely kinky behind the name.

LAWN, NEWFOUNDLAND

The grass decidedly *isn't* greener in the town of Lawn since the collapse of the fisheries industry. This village at the south end of the Burin Peninsula was first mentioned by Captain James Cook. Possible explanations for its name are that French fishermen called it *l'ane*, meaning donkey, or possibly the intrepid Cook was simply impressed by the lushness of the scenery.

It is best known for being the site of a 1942 disaster in which not one, not two, but *three* American Navy ships all ran aground nearby, causing the deaths of 203 sailors.

LEADING TICKLES, NEWFOUNDLAND

We all know what tickling can lead to, but this isn't always the case considering the birth rate of Leading Tickles has been on a downward trend for the past couple generations and the town's current population is barely over 400. "Tickle" is a term for a treacherous channel of seawater that is apparently only used in Newfoundland and Labrador, where it appears in more than 200 place names. Some of the more tickling tickles include Pinchgut Tickle, Blind Mugford Tickle, Jigger Tickle, Headforemost Tickle and Ingarggarnekulluk Tickle.

LITTLE SELDOM, NEWFOUNDLAND

There really isn't much to Seldom, a small community on Notre Dame Bay, and even less to the neighbouring community of Little Seldom. The towns only had a combined population of around 400 souls at the last count.

LOWER ECONOMY, NOVA SCOTIA

The name for this small town is practically begging for some sort of cheap shot about the collapse of the fisheries industry, but the name is actually completely unrelated to its financial decline. Originally called *Ville Conomie* by the Acadians, the name is taken from the Mi'kmaq word *Kenomee*, meaning "large point jutting into the sea," likely a reference to Minas Basin's Economy Point.

Having said that, it still probably isn't what you'd call a great place to look for a job.

MAIN-À-DIEU, NOVA SCOTIA

The name of this Cape Breton fishing village on the Marconi Trail translates from the French as "Hand of God," which is unintentionally ironic given that the name originally came from the Mi'kmaq word *menadou*, meaning an evil spirit, possibly a reference to several early shipwrecks.

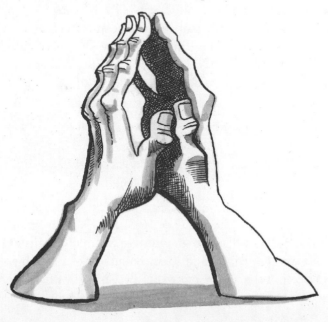

MEAT COVE, NOVA SCOTIA

Meat Cove is literally the end of the road on Cape Breton Island. Accessible only via an unpaved road off the Cabot Trail, this tiny community likely got its name from fishing fleets that used to use its protected cove to come ashore to hunt for dining alternatives to fish.

Meat Cove unexpectedly found itself in the public eye after appearing in the American syndicated comic strip *Get Fuzzy*, in which the main characters visit the village while on vacation to meet the parents of Satchel Pooch, a pun-prone anthropomorphic Labrador/Shar Pei cross, who was supposedly born there. Unfortunately, even though Satchel enjoyed his time in Meat Cove, it apparently wasn't quite as meaty as he had hoped it would be.

MECHANIC SETTLEMENT, NEW BRUNSWICK

If you find yourself broken down in the Mechanic Settlement area and need a good mechanic, you're likely going to be out of luck. According to reallymadeincanada.com, which lists every licensed auto service garage in the country, this small village in Kings County doesn't have a single one—just another case of false advertising. At least Sussex isn't too far to get towed to.

MUSHABOOM, NOVA SCOTIA

Tucked in the woods and out of sight…
On a little road barely on the map

–Feist, "Mushaboom"

This tiny fishing village on the Eastern Shore not far from Halifax unexpectedly found itself the subject of a hit single by Nova Scotia-born singer/songwriter Leslie Feist, who chose the village name to pun the doo-wop refrain "shaboom." If you've

seen the video for the song and thought the setting didn't look remotely like a remote Nova Scotia fishing village, you're right—it was shot on a street in Paris.

NAMELESS COVE, NEWFOUNDLAND

Nameless Cove, a small town on the northwestern side of the Great Northern Peninsula, got its "name" after the slightly larger nearby community of Flower's Cove stole the name "Flower's Cove" back when the Newfoundland government first began keeping track of its settlements. Flower's Cove used to be known as French Island Harbour, but after the French left, they needed a new name and simply took the closest one.

NECUM TEUCH, NOVA SCOTIA

Pronounced "nee-comm-taw," this small community near Ecum Secum received its unusual name from the Mi'kmaq word *noogoomkeak*, meaning "a beach with soft sand." Necum Teuch is famous for having dozens of realistic scarecrows created by local children's author Angela Geddes, whose kiddie lit oeuvre includes *The Scarecrows of Necum Teuch* and *Necum Teuch Notes*.

NEW DENMARK, NEW BRUNSWICK

Centuries after the Vikings first landed in northern Newfoundland, Atlantic Canada faced a second wave of invasion from the Norsemen. Fortunately, this time the Norse came to the Northeast simply to grow potatoes rather than to rape and/or pillage. Their motivation for coming again is unclear—perhaps there was a particular stench in Denmark at the time, or maybe they wanted to be able to draw cartoons of the prophet Mohammed in peace—but these Danish settlers first

started arriving in 1872, settling on the sleepy banks of the Saint John River in northern New Brunswick. North America's first Danish settlement soon became its largest when more came to join them, and even today it isn't uncommon to hear the Danish language spoken in local cafés over coffee and danishes (or, as the Danish locals call them, *wienerbrød*).

One of the settlement's main attractions is the Immigrant House, the dreary building in which the original settlers endured their first Canadian winter, which is now a Provincial Historical Site.

NIGADOO, NEW BRUNSWICK

The Mi'kmaq origin for the name of this village and river that flows into Baie des Chaleurs near the city of Bathurst translates as "hiding place," which the Acadian founders certainly needed back when the British troops were rounding them up and shipping them off. And it's fun to say out loud too.

PARADISE, NEWFOUNDLAND

Take me down to Paradise City where the grass is green and the girls are pretty.

–Guns N' Roses, "Paradise City"

Stats Canada has declared this bedroom community of St. John's to be the fastest-growing municipality in Atlantic Canada. This may not qualify it as being an actual "paradise" but, in Newfoundland, anywhere that more people are moving *to* rather than *away from* is considered a good thing. The acronym for Town of Paradise is even "T.O.P.," making it a top spot by any measure.

PISQUID, PRINCE EDWARD ISLAND

The name for this tiny village, as well as the adjacent Pisquid River, is derived from the Mi'kmaq word *Pesigitk*, which means "forks of a river."

An unincorporated area in the central part of the island, Pisquid was the setting for what was perhaps the world's largest pork roast in 1997, when a barn fire at Apple Farms accidentally killed 3500 hogs.

PLEASANTVILLE, NEWFOUNDLAND

If the Canadian military would like to be taken more seriously, it should really stop putting its military bases in places with names like "Pleasantville" and "Happy Valley-Goose Bay." This area north of Quidi Vidi Lake in St. John's was the former site of the United States military base Fort Pepperell during World War II and is now home to a reserve base of the Canadian Armed Forces. Pleasantville isn't paradise (Paradise is a few kilometres to the east), but at least it is pleasant.

POKEMOUCHE, NEW BRUNSWICK

While it sounds like some sort of Franglais mishmash describing the poking of a fly, this town on the Acadian Peninsula and the river of the same name are so-called after the Mi'kmaq word *Pocomooch*, meaning "salt water extending inward."

Pokemouche is also the headquarters of Atlantic Fine Yarns, the biggest spinning mill in Canada.

PUGWASH, NOVA SCOTIA

One of the great things I hope to accomplish is to get people of different faiths, different nationalities and different tongues to get together and find they are actually brothers after all.

–Cyrus Eaton (1883–1979)

While the name Pugwash may evoke thoughts of some sort of pet grooming business specializing in small dogs with squashed faces, this small community in Cumberland County named after a Mi'kmaq word for "deep harbour" is rather, as their billboards remind you, "world famous for peace."

Pugwash was the site of a pivotal 1957 meeting of international intellectual heavyweights who were there to state their staunch opposition to the use of nuclear weapons. The event was hosted on the estate of Pugwash's most famous native son, steel tycoon

Cyrus Eaton, and was inspired by a 1955 anti-war manifesto that had been issued by scientist Albert Einstein and philosopher Bertrand Russell and signed by no less than 10 Nobel Laureates. The manifesto called upon world leaders to give peace a chance, stating: "Shall we put an end to the human race; or shall mankind renounce war?"

The inaugural conference in Pugwash inspired a global movement and was organized by Russell and Joseph Rotblat, famed for being the only nuclear physicist to walk away from the Manhattan Project over the immorality of using science to build weapons of mass destruction.

The Pugwash Conferences went on to play a major role in the development of the Non-Proliferation Treaty of 1968 and the Anti-Ballistic Missile Treaty of 1972. They also helped to maintain open lines of communication during the Cold War and, in 1995, Rotblat and the Pugwash Conferences on Science and World Affairs were jointly awarded the Nobel Peace Prize for their efforts in nuclear disarmament.

QUIRPON, NEWFOUNDLAND

Pronounced "car-poon," Quirpon is a picturesque village on the northern tip of the Great Northern Peninsula that has the most northerly sheltered harbour on the island. Jacques Cartier himself, trapped by icebergs, was stuck in Quirpon for a few weeks in 1534, back when the place was known as "Karpont" because of its resemblance to the port of Le Kerpont, France.

QUISPAMSIS, NEW BRUNSWICK

It never occurred to me that there was anything particularly weird about having attended a school named Kennebecasis Valley High in a town called Quispamsis until I started filling out application forms and found that there was never enough space to write it all in. "Quispam," as this large suburb of Saint John is generally known, is derived from the Mi'kmaq words *quispam* ("lake") and *sis* ("little") in honour of the suitably smallish Ritchie Lake.

ROACHVILLE, NEW BRUNSWICK

A bit like Beersville (see above), this village west of Sussex doesn't live up to its name either, only here that's a good thing. Roachville is named for the descendants of early settler John Roach, who was the first settler in the 1780s, rather than for cockroaches or the remains of joints.

RIVER OF PONDS, NEWFOUNDLAND

While not as famous as Newfoundland's other paradoxical wet spot, Western Brook Pond, River of Ponds is considered to be one of the premier salmon fishing destinations in the province. Or, more specifically, River of Ponds *Stream*, which runs through the town of River of Ponds, is considered to be one of the premier salmon fishing rivers in the province.

This small town, located about 250 kilometres north of Corner Brook, is also notable for being the first community in the country to do away with municipal property taxes, opting instead to charge a flat rate fee to all residents regardless of the size of their residences, which, in River of Ponds, are admittedly mostly on the modest side to begin with. Because of this amendment, River of Ponds—which has a population hovering around 300—saves a whopping $5000 a year that previously had to be handed over the provincial government for property assessments.

SAINT JOHN, NEW BRUNSWICK/ ST. JOHN'S, NEWFOUNDLAND

A sizable chunk of Canadians remain blissfully unaware that two of the three largest cities in Atlantic Canada are actually separate places, though it's hard to blame them, really.

The largest city in New Brunswick, Saint John takes its name from being at the mouth of the St. John River, which was first discovered by Samuel de Champlain on June 24, 1604—the Feast day of St. John the Baptist. You might have also noticed that the city's "Saint" is spelled out while the river's "St." is abbreviated, which only adds to the confusion. The early settlement was split between Parr Town on the east side of the harbour and Carleton of the west and was united to form Saint John when Loyalists arrived en masse in 1785, making it Canada's first incorporated city.

KRRR...

Meanwhile, John Cabot also supposedly discovered Newfoundland's capital city of St. John's on the Feast day of St. John the Baptist in 1497—over a century before Champlain's discovery—but, since Saint John refused to cede to St. John's, they settled on using an apostrophe "s" and the abbreviated spelling "St."

SOURIS, PRINCE EDWARD ISLAND

Souris is the French word for mouse, and it is more than likely that the early French settlers in this northeastern port town on Colville Bay suffered through more than a few mice infestations. Or then again, the town might've gotten its name from

Havre à l'Echouerie, meaning "barred harbour," which could've been later rendered as "Havre à la Souris."

Souris is best known for being the "Gateway to the Magdalen Islands," offering ferry service to Québec's distant archipelago.

SUNNYVALE TRAILER PARK

COLE HARBOUR, NOVA SCOTIA

Who doesn't drink too much sometimes or who doesn't have a puff from time to time? And who doesn't have problems with the people they love? This is our home. This is our community.

–Jim Lahey, Sunnyvale Trailer Park Supervisor

Ricky, Julian and Bubbles no longer live there, but the remains of what was once the most famous fictional trailer park in the world can be found at 255 Bissett Road on the grounds of the abandoned Cole Harbour Regional Rehabilitation Centre.

Trailer Park Boys was one of the most successful Canadian TV series in history, and the 2006 feature film based on the show had the highest-grossing opening weekend of any English-language Canadian film ever produced.

What started as a low-budget parody of the Fox Network's true crime show *Cops* went on to become, as they like to say of the CBC, "a part of our heritage." Showcase channel's hit mocku-mentary—based on the misadventures of three likeable dope-smoking, heavy drinking, gun-toting criminals who habitually robbed supermarkets, liquor stores and gas stations—is now, for better or for worse (probably worse), the first image that comes to mind for many people around the world when they think of Atlantic Canada.

While the first four seasons were actually filmed in Halifax area trailer parks, the final three were shot on location at a for-mer prison, which handily doubled as the actual jail that Ricky and Julian were invariably sent to in the final episode of each season. During filming, most of the cast and crew lived in the makeshift trailer park, which can still be seen from space in all its former glory using Google Earth.

TATAMAGOUCHE, NOVA SCOTIA

This village in Colchester County is located on the Northumberland Strait between Truro and Pictou. It gets its euphonious name from the Mi'kmaq word *Takumegooch*, meaning "meeting of the waters," and had the bad luck of being the very first Acadian community to have its inhabitants forcibly expelled by the British.

The town is best known as being the former home of famed giantess Anna Swan (1846–1888), who stood around 241 centi-metres tall and who was once a star attraction at the Barnum and Bailey Circus.

Tatamagouche's next most famous citizen is multi-millionaire Ron Joyce, the co-founder of Tim Horton's, who took over after the franchise's iconic namesake died while driving drunk. Following his retirement from the doughnut biz, Joyce opened the world-famous Fox Harb'r Golf Course outside town.

More recently, Tatamagouche found itself the subject of national attention by hosting season two of the CBC series *The Week The Women Went.*

TILTING, NEWFOUNDLAND

Many of the houses and structures in Tilting are, in fact, tilting. Designated a National Cultural Landscape District of Canada, this ancient town on the eastern end of Fogo Island is renowned for its collection of traditional Irish structures, both original and restored, many of which have a distinct tilt to them. Ironically, the town gets its name from get an even earlier type of structure that is more like a lean-to—a temporary shelter made of a bark, seal skin, branches and even sails—used by early fishermen.

TOO GOOD ARM, NEWFOUNDLAND

An outport fishing community located on New World Island, Too Good Arm is distinguished not only by its funny name but also for being the hometown of a fisherman whose luck wasn't too good either. The 49-year-old inshore fisherman became the first Newfoundlander in history to be charged for jigging cod to feed his family after the federal moratorium was declared in 1994.

ULVA, NOVA SCOTIA

There is a classic episode of *Seinfeld* in which Jerry forgets the name of the woman he is dating and only knows that it rhymes with a certain part of the female anatomy. He and George come up with several possible candidates: Aretha (urethra), Celeste (breast), Bovary (ovary) and Jerry ultimately makes the wrong guess with Mulva. (For the record, her name was Dolores.)

Of course, Ulva also rhymes with a certain anatomical feature, but this happenstance had nothing to do with how this village in the Margaree Valley of Cape Breton got its name. Ulva happens to be the name of an island off the coast of Argyllshire in Scotland, and many of this area's early settlers emigrated from near there.

YANKEETOWN, NOVA SCOTIA

For obvious reasons, there isn't much "Yankee Go Home!" graffiti in this rural community just outside of Halifax; nor, for that matter, are there many Americans residing here.

Peculiar Place Names—They Called It What Now?

Of course, the cities, fishing villages and other settlements are far from the only places with weird names. Geographical features and bodies of water also provide no shortage of tongue-twisters, head-scratchers and rib-ticklers worthy of consideration.

ANNIEOPSQUOTCH MOUNTAINS, NEWFOUNDLAND

Located in the middle of the Rock between Victoria Lake and Red Indian Lake, this mountain range was formed from 500-million-year-old rock from the ocean floor and is named for a Mi'kmaq word meaning "rocky mountains." Unfortunately, the more easily pronounced "Rocky Mountains" had already been taken by a more prominent range out west. The summit of the highest of the Annieopsquotches is a modest 687 metres, while the rockiest Rocky is 4401 metres.

ANTELOPE HARBOUR, NEWFOUNDLAND

While there are moose and even caribou roaming the wilds of Newfoundland, there aren't any antelope or deer on the island, not even in the zoos. Instead, this harbour on the east side of Chateau Bay got its name from an international incident that took place during the American Revolution. A British warship, the *HMS Antelope*, intercepted an American ship, the *Mercury*, just off the coast of Labrador. The Americans, spooked, chucked a package they were carrying overboard, but a quick-thinking sailor from the *Antelope* dove in and rescued it. The package contained the details of secret negotiations the United States had been conducting with Holland.

AVALON PENINSULA, NEWFOUNDLAND

One of the first spots in North America to be inhabited by Europeans, this southeastern peninsula is now home to roughly half of Newfoundland's total population. It was named by Sir George Calvert in 1623 for the mythical site of Arthurian legend where Christianity was first introduced to England. Calvert had hoped to make the area a colony for Roman Catholics facing persecution in England, but he found the Newfoundland winters to be far more persecutory than anything the Protestants could dream up. Calvert soon gave up on his dream and hightailed it out of there for "some other warmer climate in the New World," which turned out to be Maryland. The fog-bound peninsula gives an entirely new meaning to "the Mists of Avalon."

BAIE-DES-CHALEURS, NEW BRUNSWICK

Northern New Brunswick might not be where you'd expect to find a place whose name means "Bay of Heat," but it can actually be quite nice here in July, the month during which explorer Jacques Cartier sailed into town in 1534 and described the area as being "more temperate than Spain." Nowadays, the area is best known for being a good place to keep an eye out for a flaming phantom ship, which has been spotted so often that an artist's impression of it is part of the logo for the local tourism authority.

Baie-des-Chaleurs is "hot" figuratively as well as literally and is a chartered member of the highly exclusive Most Beautiful Bays of the World Club, of which the only other Canadian bay to make the cut is Québec's Tadoussac Bay.

BIG

GARGANTUAN &
RIDICULOUSLY
OVERSIZED

Baie-des-Chaleurs is also home to the world's second-longest natural sand bar, the Eel River Bar. This sand bar is special not only because it has fresh water on one side and salt water on the other, but also because it is home to endangered birds such as bald eagles, peregrine falcons, harlequin ducks and piping plovers. Not to mention eels.

BAIE DU VIN, NEW BRUNSWICK

How is it that a non-wine-producing region of northeastern New Brunswick came to be named for what translates as "Bay of Wine" you ask? The answer, my friends, is blowing in the wind. The word *vin* has been corrupted from *vente*, which is French for "wind."

Baie du Vin also became the site of an Acadian refugee settlement after the fall of Fort Beauséjour, which gave them a legitimate reason for whining.

BLACK JOKE COVE, LABRADOR

This bay on the north shore of Belle Isle is said to have gotten its name from a pirate ship that used to hide there and has nothing to do with racist jokes, though it is just as bad an idea to drop the n-bomb here as it is anywhere else in Atlantic Canada.

BURY HEAD, PRINCE EDWARD ISLAND

This cape extending into Cascumpec Bay on the island's northern shore likely does have a head or two buried in it, though it isn't as sinister as it sounds. The point of land was known as "Berry Head" for many years after the Berry family—early settlers who, along with their heads, were planted in the old cemetery long ago. Nowadays, Bury Head is a popular bird-spotting destination for those looking to see great blue herons, bald eagles and a variety of shorebirds.

CAPE ENRAGE, NEW BRUNSWICK

Cape Enrage takes its name from a large reef that extends south into Chignecto Bay, which causes the water off the point to become extremely dangerous or, if you prefer, *enraged*. It is home to the oldest lighthouse in the province, a local landmark that sits 50 metres above the ocean. The lighthouse was at one point fully automated, but the government finally turned off the lights for good in 1988.

The property was at first scheduled for demolition, but in 1993, a group of enterprising students from Moncton's Harrison Trimble High School, working under the supervision of their physics teacher Dennison Tate, began a restoration project at the site. Successive hard-working students have since turned it into a successful tourist trap that offers climbing, rappelling and kayaking classes to the public.

Frommer's travel guide declared the view from Cape Enrage to be "the best view in Canada," beating out the popular panorama offered at St. John's Signal Hill and the sweeping vistas found at the end of the Bonavista Peninsula.

CAPE NEGRO, NOVA SCOTIA

Nobody has gotten around to changing this rather politically incorrect leftover from the olden days, despite Nova Scotia having been the last stop of the Underground Railway for escaping African-American slaves. This cape on the Atlantic Coast between Barrington Bay and Shelburne was actually named by Samuel de Champlain for its black rocks, not people.

CHRISTMAS MOUNTAINS, NEW BRUNSWICK

This festively-named mountain range is a series of 10 rounded peaks located near Mount Carleton, the province's highest peak. The Christmas Mountains were christened in 1964 after a surveyor, Arthur Wightman, noted that the previously unnamed hills lay near the fountainhead of the North Pole Stream, a small creek so-named because of its remote distance from any settlements. Feeling in a Christmassy mood, Wightman decided to give each mountain a thematic name: North Pole Mountain, Mount Dasher, Mount Dancer, Mount Prancer, Mount Vixen, Mount Comet, Mount Cupid, Mount Donder, Mount Blitzen and, last but not least, Mount St. Nicholas.

He wanted to call the final peak Mount Rudolph but the red-nosed-reindeer name was vetoed by grinches at the Canadian Permanent Committee on Geographical Names (CPCGM), who deemed it "too commercial." At the time, Rudolph was a relative newcomer to the Santa scene, having only been dreamt up 15 years earlier by the Montgomery Ward retail chain as a promotional gimmick to sell more toys.

Of course, it was a doomed effort on the CPCGM's part to try to keep Rudolph the Red-nosed Reindeer from going down in history. Or, for that matter, to try and keep the Christmas Mountains from becoming commercialized.

In the early 1990s, aerial photos revealed the remote area as having the last substantial old-growth forest in northeastern North America. The provincial Department of Natural Resources then made the hugely unpopular decision to lease the land to an American pulp and paper company, who promptly clear-cut most of the area within a few years.

CORONARY LAKE, NEW BRUNSWICK

While it's probably not a good idea to dive in headfirst after the first spring thaw, there's no actual record of fatal heart attacks at this small lake east of the Lepreau River. Instead, it is named for Ireland's Coroneary Lake, but somehow the correct spelling got lost in the wash.

CRABBE MOUNTAIN, NEW BRUNSWICK

The smallish mountain isn't shaped like a crab or even crawling with crabs. Instead, the province's biggest ski resort, located 30 minutes north of Fredericton, is named for the Crabbe family, early residents of nearby Lower Hainesville. No word on if any of the Crabbe's were skiers or were particularly crabby by nature.

Cut Throat Island, Labrador

While it may sound like this was perhaps the secret refuge of murderous pirates—the very reason a bad Geena Davis pirate movie had the same name—the cut throats in question only belonged to codfish as centuries ago this island was a busy fish-curing station.

Fogo Island, Newfoundland

The largest of Newfoundland's offshore islands, Fogo probably derived its name from the Portugese *Y do Fogo*, or "isle of fire," perhaps because of forest fires, the smoke from Beothuk campfires that early European fishermen would see coming from the island, or simply because Fogo has fog that looks like smoke. On French maps between the 16th and 18th centuries, the island is referred to as *Île des Fougues*.

FOLLY LAKE, NOVA SCOTIA

Folly Lake, along with lesser-known Folly Mountain and Folly River, takes its name from the folly of an early Scottish settler named James Flemming, who decided to try his luck by farming on a notoriously stony chunk of land. The settlement came to be known as "Flemming's Folly" before eventually being changed to the more sensible-sounding Glenholme.

GIN HILL, NEW BRUNSWICK

Located near Nason Brook in northern Victoria County, Gin Hill is named for a boozy 19th-century incident in which a couple of workers overturned their carriage on the hill. The accident caused the full case of gin they were transporting to crack open after their panicked horses ran off. By the time a rescue party eventually found them, there apparently wasn't much gin left to salvage.

GROS MORNE NATIONAL PARK, NEWFOUNDLAND

The second-largest national park in Atlantic Canada is named for Newfoundland's second-highest mountain, the 806-metre Gros Morne, a name that, translated poetically from the French, means "large mountain standing alone" or, more literally, "big gloomy." A UNESCO World Heritage Site, the park provides a rare example of the process of continental drift thanks to the exposure of deep ocean crust and rocks of the earth's mantle.

HA HA BAY, NEWFOUNDLAND

Ha ha!

–Nelson Muntz, *The Simpsons*

The story behind Ha Ha Bay isn't as funny as you might imagine. The term "ha ha" is actually an archaic French term meaning "an unexpected obstacle," or *cul de sac*. In this case, a sand bar in the inlet acts as an obstruction to the larger Piscolet Bay. There's also a Ha Ha Point and a Ha Ha Mountain, though the community of Ha Ha itself was renamed Raleigh for a Royal Navy cruiser that ran aground there in 1922. Eleven sailors drowned in the shipwreck, which isn't very funny either.

There are several similarly named places in Québec, the best known being the peculiarly punctuated Saint-Louis-du-Ha! Ha!

Recently, Raleigh has rallied many international botanical experts to it after several new species of plants were discovered in the area, plants that are found nowhere else on earth. Located near the tip of the Great Northern Peninsula and surrounded on three sides by the cold waters of the Strait of Belle Isle, the peninsula of nearby Burnt Cape has some of the most arctic conditions on the Rock, allowing for 300 unique northern plant species to thrive.

KEJIMKUJIK NATIONAL PARK, NOVA SCOTIA

"Keji" is Atlantic Canada's only inland national park. Located in the western Nova Scotia wilderness, the 404-square-kilometre park is famous for its canoe routes that were once used as shortcuts by the Mi'kmaq to get between the Bay of Fundy and the South Shore. In fact, the park takes its name from the Mi'kmaq word *koojumkoojik*, possibly meaning "chafed testicles"—the result of long days spent paddling and portaging through the region—though the National Parks Board stubbornly insists that the word actually means "tired muscles."

A famous book by Albert Paine called *The Tent Dwellers*, publishing in 1908, is about fishing in Kejimkujik for "abounding Nova Scotia trout" with two Native guides. Sadly, the trout are now almost entirely gone thanks to the effects of imported acid rain.

KOUCHIBOUGUAC NATIONAL PARK, NEW BRUNSWICK

Pronounced "kou-che-boo-gwack," the name is taken from the Mi'kmaq word *Pijeboogwek* meaning "the river of long tides," which refers to one or both of the two rivers that run through the park, the Black and the Kouchibouguacis. Located on the east coast near the town of Richibucto, "Koochee" was founded in 1969 to preserve its sensitive sand dunes and tidal flats. The 238-square-kilometre park is home to the endangered piping plover (*Charadrius melodus*) and the second-largest tern colony in North America. Hundreds of harbour and grey seals also call the park home during the summer months, and sea lions can often be spotted soaking up the sun on the sand dunes.

LOWER NORTH BRANCH OF THE LITTLE SOUTHWEST MIRAMICHI RIVER, NEW BRUNSWICK

The Mi'kmaq take a fair bit of ribbing for their multi-syllabic mouthfuls for place names but, in all fairness, it's worth mentioning that they simply called this river *Megamaage*, or "land of the Mi'kmaq."

The Lower North Branch of the Little Southwest Miramichi River is only the ninth-longest place name in Canada, well behind both the aforementioned Newfoundland community of "Cape St. George-Petit Jardin-Grand Jardin-De Grau-Marches Point-Loretto" and the PEI community listed in the books as "Stanley Bridge, Hope River, Bayview, Cavendish and North Rustico."

This popular salmon fishing river has its headwaters at Gover Lake in the Appalachian Mountains and joins the Northwest Miramichi River at the village of Red Bank and later the Southwest Miramichi River in Newcastle to form the plain-old Miramichi for the rest of its way to the sea.

MALIGNANT COVE, NOVA SCOTIA

Malignant Cove is not the most inviting name for this otherwise-picturesque place on the Northumberland coast. Despite two official attempts to change the name to something less evil-sounding—including one in 1915 by the Nova Scotia Legislature suggesting it be change to "Milburn"— Malignant it has always been and Malignant it remains. The cove was named for the British warship *HMS Malignant* which, possibly jinxed by its unlucky name, ran aground here in 1774.

MASSACRE ISLAND, NOVA SCOTIA

There are two versions to explain how this small island off Port Mouton got its slaughterous name. One is that a French ship was wrecked here and the survivors were subsequently murdered by Mi'kmaq. Another version says the workers who built the mysterious tunnels of the Oak Island Money Pit (see Interesting Islands) were brought here after they'd finished their excavations and were brutally executed to preserve the island's booty-licious secret. A number of scattered human remains have been found here over the centuries, which lends credence to either version.

NAKED MAN HILL, NEWFOUNDLAND

Merasheen Island's Naked Man Hill is famous for its erections, piles of stones or "naked men," first put up by Captain James Cook when he built a base of operations on the island's summit while surveying Placentia Bay.

PISSING MARE FALLS, NEWFOUNDLAND

The name for the tallest waterfall in eastern North America may not be very PC, but at least it has the "Pee." The falls, at 350-metres high, are among the highest in eastern North America and drop from Big Level Plateau into Western Brook Pond in Gros Morne National Park.

There are two theories as to the colourful name. One is that the waterfall resembles the steady stream of a urinating female horse, and the other is that "Mare" has been corrupted from the original *mer*, French for "sea," which the enormous Western Brook Pond resembles (and was actually once a part of—more on this below).

Swimmers and thirsty hikers can rest assured that the water in the fjord has been assigned the highest purity rating available for natural bodies of water.

PULL AND BE DAMNED NARROWS/PUSH AND BE DAMNED RAPIDS, NEW BRUNSWICK

There are a total of three local variations in New Brunswick on the futility of trying to row or paddle against strong currents. Pull and Be Damned Narrows can be properly experienced during ebb tide in the Letang River near the town of St. George, while two separate Push and Be Damned Rapids can be found, one on the Nepisiguit River and one on the Southwest Miramichi River.

RANDOM SOUND, NEWFOUNDLAND

The name for this body of water on the west side of Trinity Bay probably wasn't chosen at random or for an arbitrary noise. "Random" can be traced to the old English word *randan*, meaning "mayhem" or "riotous behaviour," and nearby Random Island could well have once been the setting of a particularly chaotic drinking binge.

SKEDADDLE RIDGE, NEW BRUNSWICK

Now known as Pemberton Ridge, this hill in York County on the border with Maine was a popular escape route for Americans wanting to dodge the draft during the American Civil War and "skedaddle" into Canada. It might've been used the same way once or twice during the Vietnam War as well.

SISSIBOO RIVER, NOVA SCOTIA

The current Digby County town of Weyburn on the Sissiboo River used to be called Sissiboo as well, but the name was deemed too ridiculous. The name is likely from either the Mi'kmaq word *cibou* meaning "big," or it has something to do with seeing six owls, which in French would be the similar sounding *six hiboux.*

SODOM LAKE, NOVA SCOTIA

I bent over backward trying to track down the story behind this lake, but despite all my anal research into the matter, I couldn't find bugger all about it. But I'm sure hoping it has something to do with some sort of fishermen's version of Brokeback Mountain.

WESTERN BROOK POND, NEWFOUNDLAND

The world-famous Western Brook Pond is neither a brook nor a pond, though to be fair to whoever named it, it is located in the western part of the island. One of the main attractions of Gros Morne National Park, Western Brook Pond is a unique freshwater fjord surrounded by steep rock walls that was initially carved out by glaciers and then was left stranded a few kilometres inland when the ice melted.

ABOUT THE AUTHOR

Andrew Fleming

Andrew Fleming grew up in southern New Brunswick. He has a perfectly sensible B.A. in English from McGill University and is slowly getting used to being mistaken for the more famous Andrew Fleming who wrote such films as *Hamlet 2* and *The Craft*. He is a writer and a copyeditor for local newspapers, a bartender and a raft guide. This is his third book.

ABOUT THE ILLUSTRATORS

Peter Tyler

Peter is a recent graduate of the Vancouver Film School's Visual Art and Design and Classical animation programs. Though his ultimate passion is in filmmaking, he is also intent on developing his draftsmanship and storytelling, with the aim of using those skills in future filmic misadventures.

Roger Garcia

Roger Garcia is a self-taught artist with some formal training who specializes in cartooning and illustration. He is an immigrant from El Salvador, and during the last few years, his work has been primarily cartoons and editorial illustrations in pen and ink. Recently he has started painting once more. Focusing on simplifying the human form, he uses a bright minimal palette and as few elements as possible. His work can be seen in newspapers, magazines, promo material and on www.rogergarcia.ca

Patrick Hénaff

Born in France, Patrick Hénaff is mostly self-taught. He is a versatile artist who has explored a variety of media under many different influences. He now uses primarily pen and ink to draw and then processes the images on computer. He is particularly interested in the narrative power of pictures and tries to use them as a way to tell stories.

Pat Bidwell

Pat has always had a passion for drawing and art. Initially self-taught, Pat completed art studies in visual communication in 1986. Over the years, he has worked both locally and internationally as an illustrator/product designer and graphic designer, collecting many awards for excellence along the way. When not at the drawing board, Pat pursues other interests solo and/or with his wife, Lisa.

Graham Johnson

Graham Johnson is an illustrator and graphic designer. When he isn't drawing or designing, he...well...he's always drawing or designing! On the off-chance you catch him not doing one of those things, he's probably cooking, playing tennis or poring over other illustrations.

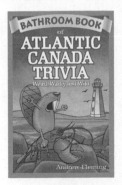

**BATHROOM BOOK OF
ATLANTIC CANADA TRIVIA**
Weird, Wacky and Wild
by Andrew Fleming
The east coast of Canada has a history and distinct cultural flavour like no other, and that makes for a gold mine of fascinating trivia. Discover the East Coaster who created the Academy Awards, the prime minister who is distantly related to the Trailer Park Boys and the disturbing rumours around the founding of our nation.

$9.95 • ISBN: 978-1-897278-21-5 • 5.25" x 8.25" • 168 pages

WHAT IS CANADA?
The Ultimate Canadian Quiz Book
by Dan de Figueiredo
Test your knowledge on Canadian quotes, emblems, holidays, history, words, language, sports, geography, science, arts, entertainment, literature, crime and First Nations.

$18.95 • ISBN: 978-1-897278-50-5 • 5.25" x 8.25" • 392 pages

BATHROOM BOOK OF CANADIAN TRIVIA
by Angela Murphy
Just the facts, ma'am...just the facts.... That's what you will enjoy in *Bathroom Book of Canadian Trivia*—an entertaining and lighthearted collection of illustrated factoids from across the country.

$9.95 • ISBN: 978-0-9739116-0-2 • 5.25" x 8.25" • 144 pages